Best Sights to See at
Indiana Dunes
National Park

By Rob Bignell

Atiswinic Press · Ojai, Calif.

BEST SIGHTS TO SEE AT INDIANA DUNES NATIONAL PARK

A GUIDEBOOK IN THE BEST SIGHTS TO SEE SERIES

Copyright Rob Bignell, 2019

Atiswinic Press
Ojai, Calif. 93023
dayhikingtrails.wordpress.com

ISBN 978-1-948872-05-8

Cover design by Rob Bignell
Cover photo of view from atop Mount Baldy, Indiana Dunes National Park.

Manufactured in the United States of America
First printing April 2019

For Kieran
"Summer breeze, makes me feel fine"
-Seals and Croft, "Summer Breeze"

Contents

Introduction

I magine a place where you can stroll magnificent Lake Michigan beaches and scramble over towering sand dunes, where you can explore mysterious marshes filled with carnivorous plants and amble about peaceful oak savannas, where you can roam among migrating birds on their stopover and traipse about historic turn-of-the-century homesteads. The place is real: It's called Indiana Dunes National Park.

Located in northwest Indiana on Lake Michigan's shores, Indiana Dunes became America's newest and 61st national park in February 2019. An easy drive from Chicago, Indiana Dunes attracts about 3.6 million visitors per year, making it among the 10 most visited national parks. Formerly Indiana Dunes National Lakeshore, the 15,000-acre park sits in a built-up area and is physically divided into 15 largely disconnected pieces. Still, Indiana Dunes boasts 14 distinct trail systems with more than 50 miles of trails.

Indiana Dunes' designation as a national park follows a more than century-long effort to achieve that status. As far back as 1899, calls were made to preserve this beautiful and unique Lake Michigan shoreline. In 1916, the National Park Service's first director, Stephen Mather, advocated creation of "Sand Dunes National Park" along the Lake Michigan shoreline. Industrial interests, however, fought instead for a larger port there; indeed, remnants of the steel industry remain all around the park.

Then in the early 1950s, the Save the Dunes Council under the leadership of Dorothy Buell and activist Hazel Hannell sought federal protection. When U.S. Sen. Paul H. Douglas of Illinois joined their cause, the area became a national lakeshore in 1966. Gradually, the park expanded over the next three decades.

In 2017, Indiana congressmen called for the national lakeshore to be reclassified as a park to bring it more recognition and hence economically boost the northwestern part of their state, which had suffered greatly since the decline of the steel industry and other manufacturing there. Initially, the National Park service opposed the reclassification, saying Indiana Dunes had more in common with its national lake and seashores than with a national park. Still, a bill renaming the national lakeshore soon passed Congress and was signed into law by President Donald Trump.

With the park stretching more than two-dozen miles from end to end and the large crowds, though, how can you ensure that you see its main sights when vacationing or driving through? That's what "Best Sights to See at Indiana Dunes National Park" answers. In this volume, we've listed the top 10 most popular sights and detail the top day hiking trails to best experience them.

How to Get There

With Indiana Dunes situated so close to Chicago, a number of major highways lead to the park.

Interstate 90 heads east from Chicago and west from South Bend, Indiana. Interstate 94 also enters the park as driving east from Chicago and then west from southern Michigan. Interstate 65 runs north from Indianapolis.

Most trails in the park can be accessed by roads intersecting

Indiana Dunes National Park runs along the Lake Michigan shoreline in northern Indiana. (NPS map)

either U.S. Hwy. 12 (aka as Dunes Highway) or U.S. Hwy. 20. Each runs roughly west-east between Chicago and Michigan City, Ind., right through the park's heart. Because of that, explanations of how to reach trailheads for nearly all of the featured trails begin with directions from those two cities.

If you don't want to drive, there is a great option in Chicago for reaching the park. The South Shore Line, a commuter rail line running between downtown Chicago and South Bend International Airport, includes a Dune Park stop east of Cowles Bog and south of Indiana Dunes State Park; you can pick up the

Calumet Trail at the station. From April through October, you can bring bicycles on the South Shore Line train.

When to Visit

The best months to day hike Indiana Dunes are May through September. Depending on the year, April and October also can be pleasant.

As with the rest of the Midwest, summers can be humid, especially July and August. Rain also can occur during the afternoon even when the morning is sunny, so always check the weather forecast before heading out.

November through March usually is too cold for day hiking. Once snow falls, some trails are used for cross-country skiing or snowshoeing. Early spring often means muddy trails thanks to snowmelt, rainfall and flooding.

Kids Activities

A trip to Indiana Dunes can be an educational experience for kids – though they may be having too much fun to even notice that they're learning!

The park delivers a variety of great activities that children can participate in all year. Among the many offerings:

• **Junior Ranger Kids** – Kids between the ages of 5-12 can become a Junior Ranger. They'll first need to obtain a Junior Ranger booklet (available online at *nps.gov/indu/learn/kids youth/junior-ranger-book.htm* and at the Dorothy Buell Memorial Visitor Center) and complete its activities, and then they can receive a Junior Ranger badge. Briefer Junior Ranger Activity booklets also are available for families visiting the park just for a day.

• **Summer events** – Programs throughout the year help children (and even adults) learn about plants and animals at the park. First Saturday Night Stargazing, ranger-led hikes, Campfire on the Beach, birding programs, and more are held between Memorial and Labor Day.

• **Online games** – On the way to the national park, kids can play two online games that help them learn about the park's ecology, the Web Ranger Challenge (for middle school students) and the Water Safety Challenge/Game. Visit *nps.gov/indu/learn/education/onlinegames.htm.*

Maps

To properly prepare for any hike, you should examine maps before hitting the trail and bring them with you (See Bonus Section II for more.). No guidebook can reproduce a map as well as the satellite pictures or topographical maps that you can find online for free. To that end, a companion website (*dayhikingtrails.wordpress.com/trail-maps*) to this book offers a variety of printable maps for each listed trail.

Best Sights

I ndiana Dunes National Park is so large that unless you spend several deasons there, you won't see all it offers. So when you've only a few days at best to visit the park, what are the absolute must-see sights? Following are the park's 10 best spots and the day hiking trails for getting to them, roughly from east to west.

As the Mount Baldy dune moves inland, it consumes trees along the way. NPS photo.

Dunes

Mount Baldy Trail

Day hikers can clamber to the top of a 12-story living sand dune on the Mount Baldy Summit Trail.

The 0.8-mile trail can only be accessed on a ranger-led hike but is well worth the wait. Times for the hour-long daytime and sunset treks on summer weekends are listed in the park's newspaper (*The Singing Sands*), the park's website calendar, and its Facebook page.

To reach the trailhead, from Chicago head east or from Michigan City, Ind., go west on U.S. Hwy. 12. Turn north onto Rice Street; parking lots are at the road's end. Try to find a spot in the first (westernmost) lot. From that lot's southwest corner, take the Beach Trail about 0.18 miles to a spur on the right/east side. Turn onto the spur and stop, waiting for the ranger-led hike to begin.

The 126-foot-tall sand dune on Lake Michigan's southern shore is "living," as it shifts about four feet every year. Whenever the prevailing northwest wind tops 7 mph, the beach sand moves.

Urbanization is slowly killing the sand dune, however. Thanks to a breakwall constructed decades ago for the Michigan City Harbor, the lake's waves are taking away more beach sand than they bring in. The U.S. Army Corps of Engineers since 1974 has brought in more than 85,000 cubic yards of sand to keep Mount Baldy alive.

Global warming also is starving the sand dune. The shorter and warmer winters decrease the amount of days shelf ice protects the shore from storm erosion.

Mount Baldy – and the other dunes at the national park – formed at the end of the last ice age when lakes of glacial meltwater dried up, leaving exposed sand. As currents and wind from Lake Michigan hit the shore at angles, the sand moved along the shoreline rather than eroded away. Once it reached a stream, a sandbar formed, resulting in the formation of a small bay with a wide sand spit between it and Lake Michigan.

Eventually the sand spit filled the bay's opening to the Great Lake, and a dune ridge was created. Some dunes at the national park rise 200 feet above the beach.

Marram grass and later trees stabilize the dunes so that other than the sandy ground and steep climb over them, you'd never know you were walking on a dune.

The national park has closed Mount Baldy for a couple of reasons. First, excessive walking across it has led to a loss of vegetation, so it's no longer stable and threatens to move across the parking lots. Secondly, fungus-ridden black oaks buried by the dune are decomposing, creating deep holes known as chimneys that people can fall into. A few years ago, a young child slipped into one of these void spaces and was almost buried alive.

Ranger-led tours keep hikers on a path so they do not crush any returning vegetation or fall into chimneys.

The Mount Baldy hike begins with a scramble up steep, loose sand. The path gains 55 feet elevation in very short order with a maximum grade of 13 percent. A rope can be used to pull yourself up the final stretch.

Views from atop the barren sand dune are incredible. Lake Michigan stretches across the northern horizon, and on a clear day to the northwest the downtown Chicago skyline is visible.

Those who don't want to make the hike still can experience Mount Baldy through the beach. Just follow the Beach Trail north. The trail and beach curl east along the dune's base. Marram grass and cottonwoods grow on the foredune.

Other Dunes Trails

America's newest national park is a great destination for dunes lovers. Indiana Dunes sits on the south shore of Lake Michigan, where many of the dunes formed during recent ice ages when the water levels were much higher. Today, some dunes at the park rise 20 stories above the ground.

Most of the park's dunes can be reached via a day hike:

• **Calumet Dunes Paved Trail** – This half-mile loop heads over a dunes formed 12,000 years ago during the last ice age when Glacial Lake Chicago's surface was at 620 feet above sea level, 40 feet higher than Lake Michigan's current level. The trailhead is on North Kemil Road just north of U.S. Hwy. 12 outside of Chesterton, Ind. The loop connects with the large Glenwood Dunes Trail system; to avoid getting lost, veer left at each junction. The trail is wheelchair accessible.

• **Cowles Bog Trail** – The third/westernmost loop of this 3.65-mile trail crosses high dunes for a great view of Lake Michigan. The dunes' high points actually have names – Mount Bentley at 689 feet elevation is on the the east side, and the more prominent Mount Tuthill at 758 feet on the west. Pick up the trail from the parking lot off of N. Mineral Springs Road north of Hwy. 12.

• **Dune Ridge Trail** – Sweeping views of the Great Marsh await on this forested 0.7-mile lollipop trail near Beverly Shores, Ind. Before reaching the vista, the route heads through a foredune and oak savanna. The trail starts from the lot off of East State Park Road north of Hwy. 12 with an elevation gain of 73 feet and 4 percent average grade.

• **Dunes Succession Trail** – This excellent 1-mile trail takes hikers through the four stages of dune development and offers a fantastic view of Lake Michigan and the distant Chicago skyline. Hikers have to climb 250 stairs to the vista. The trail also passes through a jack pines grove, which is among the southernmost spots these trees have settled, thanks to ice age glaciers transporting seeds here thousands of years ago. Pick up the trail from the parking lots at the end of West Beach Road north of Hwy. 12 near Ogden Dunes, Ind.

• **Glenwood Dunes Trail** – Day hikers can walk across a forested dunes on a 2.8-miles lollipop trail. Almost all of the trail passes through a hardwood forest, known for its colorful fall foliage. Among the dominant trees are eastern black oak, white oak, sugar maple, dogwood, and yellow poplar, which top a dunes rising 640 feet above sea level. The trailhead is at the parking lot off of School House Road immediately north of U.S. Hwy. 20.

• **Paul H. Douglas Trail** – This 3.2-miles trail (formerly the Miller Woods Trail) heads through an oak savanna-covered dunes. After crossing the Grand Calumet River, the trail goes over and around towering dunes on the way to a Lake Michigan beach, offering a chance for hikers to walk through loose sand. Pick up the trail from the Douglas Center for Environmental Education in eastern Gary, Ind.

• **Tolleston Dunes Trail** – There's plenty of wildlife to be seen on and around the dunes. One good spot to catch them is this 2.6-mile trail, which traverses a variety of ecosystems, including rolling sand dunes formed 4700 years ago when Lake Michigan's water level was about 25 feet higher and reached this far inland. Among the wildlife here are cottontail rabbits, garter snakes, opossums, raccoons, red fox, squirrels and white-tailed deer. Look to the sky, and you're likely to see great blue herons, hawks, mallards, turkey vultures, and a range of songbirds. The trail starts at the parking lot off of Hwy. 12 just west of Hillcrest Road near Ogden Dunes.

Majestic Birds

Great Marsh Trail

On the Great Marsh Trail, day hikers can see a number of the famous birds attracted to the national park.

The 1.26-miles lollipop trail, with a spur to the observation deck, gains a mere nine feet of elevation as it traverses a marsh alongside Lake Michigan. Thanks to a recent restoration of the wetlands, migratory birds – including sandhill cranes and great blue herons – stop over there every spring and autumn.

To reach the trailhead, from Chicago take U.S. Hwy. 12 east or from Michigan City, Ind., go west on the road. Upon reaching Beverly Shores, Ind., turn north onto Broadway Avenue. Park in the South Lot on the street's right/east side. The largely grass trail (some patches are packed dirt) heads out from the lot's east side.

The Great Marsh is an interdunal wetland, a water-filled depression between two sand dunes. It's the largest wetlands complex in the Lake Michigan watershed, stretching for several miles between Burns Harbor, Ind., and Michigan City.

At 0.3 miles, the trail comes to the first junction. Go right/east on it. The marsh is on the trail's left/north side.

You'll be immediately impressed by the array of wildlife in the Great Marsh. Coots, mallards, wood ducks and geese are abundant there. During the annual migrations, wading birds such as herons and egrets stalk the shorelines. Kingfishers, red-winged blackbirds, tree swallows, and warblers also are plentiful. Another surprise: Sometimes beavers can be spotted playing in the marsh's channels.

In 0.1 miles, the trail reaches the loop's beginning. Continue straight-right/east, which takes you onto slightly higher ground.

A great blue heron along the Great Marsh Trail. NPS photo.

Sandhill cranes are easy to pick out when they stop over on their migration. Tall and graceful, the slate gray bird has a long neck, legs and wingspan. Their wings can stretch up to 2.2 yards across from tip to tip.

After another 0.3 miles, the loop reaches its northwest corner and re-enters the marsh.

Another large migrating bird found at the Great Marsh are great blue herons. Slightly larger than sandhill cranes, the gray-blue bodied bird has a barely longer wingspan. They often wade along the shoreline picking off small fish but being opportunistic will eat everything from insects to snakes.

In 0.1 miles, the trail comes full circle. Go right/west back onto the stem trail.

Egrets – a type of heron with white plumage – also inhabit the marsh. Other than the coloring, they look virtually identical to the great blue heron. Indeed, the word "egret" comes from the French *aigrette*, which means "silver heron."

About 0.1 miles later, you'll reach another junction. Instead of continuing on the stem trail, go straight/left/west onto the boardwalk.

For almost a century, virtually none of the wetlands birds could be found here. During the early 1900s, the wetlands was drained through a series of ditches so that the land could be used for farming and housing. As the wetlands disappeared, the water table dropped, allowing trees to take over the interdunal area.

In less than 0.1 miles, the boardwalk reaches a spur leading to the observation deck. This is a great spot to break out the binoculars and camera.

The National Park Service in 1998 began restoring the wetlands. This including filling ditches and plugging culverts that drained the marshes, erecting levees with spillways, removing the non-wetlands trees, and replanting the sedges and grasses that existed in the original wetlands.

After taking in the sights, retrace your steps back to the parking lot.

Wear boots with good traction, as the trail can be muddy and slippery. No pets are allowed.

Note that the North lot is handicap parking only. A short wheelchair-accessible trail runs from the lot to the overlook of the marsh.

Other Birding Trails

Among the best places to go birding in the upper Midwest is Indiana Dunes. With its variety of ecosystems – from hardwood forests and wetlands to Lake Michigan beaches and towering dunes – the national park naturally attracts hundreds of bird species, especially during the spring and fall migrations.

Among the top park trails for birding are:

• **Cowles Bog Trail** – The trail, which traverses the edge of woodlands and marshes while heading through an oak savanna, was named a globally significant Important Bird Area. Its wetlands are a major nesting area for American bittern, American black duck, black-crowned night heron, little blue heron, marsh wren, sandhill crane, and Virginia rail. Other rare species that can ne spotted along the trail are the American woodcock, solitary sandpiper, rusty blackbird, sedge wren, and whip-poor-will. Start at the trail heading from the parking lot off of N. Mineral Springs Road north of U.S. Hwy. 12.

• **Heron Rookery Trail** – For some six decades, more than a hundred great blue heron nests could be found in the tall sycamores along this 3.3-miles round trip trail at 600 East south of 1350 North. Though the herons have since abandoned the site, plenty of other birds can be spotted on this wooded portion of the East Arm Little Calumet River. Among them are kingfishers, kinglets, a number of migrating and nesting warbler species, woodpeckers and wood thrushes.

• **West Beach Trail** – Several migratory birds rarely seen in Indiana can be seen on the West Beach Trail, which passes Long Lake and a Lake Michigan beach. An Important Bird Area, in late fall and winter, the common redpoll, long-eared owl and red crossbill can be spotted. The common loon and red-breasted merganser, red-throated loon, and western grebe also can be seen here. Many raptors such as bald eagles, northern harriers, peregrine falcon, red-shouldered and sharp-shinned hawks stop over here. Also keep an eye out for the hairy woodpecker. The trailhead is at the lot off of West Beach Road east of County Line Road At the **Portage Lakefront and Riverwalk** on West Beach's east end, spring hawk flights over the high dunes are impressive, and during March and April, at the migration's peak, up to 300 bird species can be seen on any given day. Pick up the trail from the second parking lot off of Riverwalk Drive east of Midwest Steele road.

Hardwood Forests
Glenwood Dunes Trail

Day hikers can walk through a classic Midwestern hardwood forest on the Glenwood Dunes Trail at America's newest national park.

The lollipop trail described here runs 2.8-miles round trip through Indiana Dunes. Some guidebooks and maps call the route by its old name, the Ly-co-ki-we Trail.

To reach the trailhead, from Chicago take U.S. Hwy. 12 east or from Michigan City, Ind., take that road west. At Ind. Hwy. 49, turn south then at U.S. Hwy. 20 go left/east. Upon reaching North Brummit Road/School House Road, turn left/north. The parking lot is the first left.

Look for the trailhead at the lot's western side. When the trail splits, go right/northwest. Much of the trail's surface is packed dirt or loose sand.

Almost all of the trail passes through a hardwood forest, known for its colorful fall foliage. Among the dominant trees are eastern black oak, white oak, sugar maple, dogwood, and yellow poplar.

The first section of the trail, like the rest of Indiana, is fairly flat terrain. Typical of hardwood forests across the Midwest and New England, the woods contains scattered deadfall and shrubs.

In 0.5 miles, the trail reaches a junction. Go right/north to begin the loop.

The landscape turns to gently rolling, low, wooded dunes. Among the trees that love the sandier soil is eastern black oak. It can reach a height of 82 feet and a diameter of 35 inches. Black oak sometimes can be difficult to identify as it hybridizes with red oak; in fact, more than a dozen oak species are combinations of black and red oaks.

A variety of hardwood trees grow along the Glenwood Dunes Trail. NPS photo.

This section of the trail includes a couple of short board-walks over swampy areas. It also crosses Furnessville Road. Though the road is lightly traveled, always be careful when crossing it and other highways along the way.

North of the road, you'll find American holly. It's a very rare conifer in this part of the Midwest. The holly tree usually grows about 66 feet tall with a trunk 20 inches in diameter, and its light gray bark sports small lumps. Birds love the holly's red berries.

At 0.9 miles in, the trail comes upon another junction. Go right/north on it.

This segment cuts through the edge of a wetlands while a forested sand dune rises on the left. After leaving the wetlands, part of the trail loops through the dune.

Among the trees you'll spot here is the white oak. The tree's name comes from the color of its wood; its bark actually is a light gray. It usually grows up to 100 feet high with a massive canopy supported by large branches. Mature oaks drop massive amounts of acorns, so don't be surprised to see squirrels and chipmunks scampering beneath them. White oaks can live 200 to 300 years, though some are known to be around 600 years old.

About 1.45 miles from the trailhead, the path reaches another junction with a cut-off that heads to the other side of the loop and was previously passed on the hike. Avoid the cut-off and go right/southwest.

White-tailed deer are common in hardwood forests, and sightings of them often have occurred on this segment of the trail. They can grow around three-feet high at the shoulder and weigh up to 200 pounds. Should you spot a deer, unless it is in the distance or freezes, don't expect to see it for long. Despite long skinny legs, they can run up to 40 miles per hour, jump nine feet high (allowing them to clear almost any fence), and can swim about 13 miles per hour. When broad jumping, they can leap up to 30 feet in a single bound.

After crossing the road E 1500 N, you'll arrive at another junction, about 1.75 miles in. Go straight-left/south.

The trail curls back toward the parking lot, crossing the road N 200 E along the way. This entire segment is forested.

Especially if walking in autumn, you're sure to notice the sugar maple, popular first for its seasonal leaf color – which changes from summer's deep green to fall's yellow, orange, red and then a dark burgundy – and of course, for its sweet maple syrup that tastes perfect on pancakes, waffles and French toast. The tree reaches heights of 80-115 feet and is easily identifiable by its distinctive leaf, seen on the Canadian flag. Sugar maples can live up to 400 years.

In spring, you're likely to spot the dogwood tree thanks to

its showy white flowers. It's a popular ornamental tree because of those blossoms and its fascinating bark patterns. Dogwoods grow about 33 feet high with a trunk diameter of up to a foot.

Another interesting tree along this segment is the yellow poplar, also known as a tulip tree. It's so nicknamed because its flowers resemble that of the tulip, but it's actually a type of a magnolia. Yellow poplars grow to an immense size, sometimes exceeding 164 feet in height and more than five feet around, dwarfing the mature white oaks and sugar maples around them.

At 2.3 miles, the loop reaches the stem trail. Go right/east onto it and retrace your steps back to the parking lot.

The hike easily can be extended as a number of trails connect to the route described here. The connecting Calumet Dunes Paved Trail, Dunewood Trace Campground Trail, and Glenwood Dunes Extension Trail provide for nearly 15 miles of hiking.

In addition, the trail is equestrian friendly. Always step aside for passing horses and keep an eye out for their occasional gift left on the trail.

Other Hardwood Forests Trails

Say "Indiana Dunes," and most people will think of Lake Michigan beaches and sand dunes. But various forests – from Midwest hardwoods to a jack pinery – also can be found there.

The best trails to explore the national park's forests include:

• **Calumet Dunes Paved Trail** – The 0.5-miles loop heads through a hardwood forest on its way to sand dunes. Among the dominant trees are eastern black oak, white oak, sugar maple, dogwood, and yellow poplar, making for colorful fall foliage. If walking the trail clockwise, always veer right at each junction. The wheelchair accessible path connects with the

Glenwood Dunes Trail and the Dunewood Trace Campground Trail. Park in the lot for the trail off of East 300 Road south of U.S. Hwy. 12.

• **Dune Succession Trail** – While much of the trail focuses on how the dunes evolve over time, one segment of the 1-mile hike heads through a jack pinery. The jack pines here are much farther south than they should be in the Great Lakes. In the pinery, you'll also see cottonwood, red cedar, common juniper, and the bearberry bush. Park in a lot at the end of West Beach Road north of U.S. Hwy. 12.

• **Hobart Woodland Trail** – The 2.2-miles trail runs through forested ravines and a bur oak savanna as well as passes Lake George in the Hobart Prairie Grove System, which is disconnected from the main park. The best way to access the trail is to park at Robinson Lake Park lot off of Liverpool Road south of West 49th Avenue southwest of Hobart, Ind., then hike the Oak Savannah rail trail east for just under a half mile. The packed dirt Hobart Woodland Trail heads south from the Oak Savannah Trail.

Mysterious Marshes
Cowles Bog Trail

Day hikers can explore one of the national park's many mysterious marshes via the Cowles Bog Trail.

The 2.85-miles round trip hike is a segment of two stacked loops created by the Cowles Bog and the Greenbelt trails. This segment consists of a stem trail and the entire first loop, keeping the walk focused on Cowles Bog by leaving out a steep sand dune and the Lake Michigan beach.

Cowles Bog actually is a fen, long known in literature as a dismal place; in the ancient Anglo-Saxon tale of *Beowulf*, the frightening, fog-laden fen was the lair of the monster Grendel. At Cowles, the mineral-rich groundwater feeds the wetlands, where partially decomposed plants settle into a mire and form peat. Unlike the nearby Pinhook Bog, Cowles' water isn't acidic but quite alkaline.

To reach the trailhead, from Chicago head east on U.S. Hwy. 12 or from Michigan City, Ind., go west on the road. Near Porter, Ind., turn north onto N. Mineral Springs Road. Just before passing the Town of Dune Acres guardhouse, go right/east into the Cowles Bog Trail parking area. Walk alongside the parking lot entry road back to the guardhouse and cross N. Mineral Springs Road. The trail heads west from there.

The first segment – a stem trail – cuts between an uplands on the right/north and the Cowles Bog on the left/south.

Red maple and yellow birch dominate the uplands, but paper birch, tamarack and white pine also can be found. The fen along the first part of the stem trail often is referred to as a tamarack swamp because of the trees growing in it.

Along the bog's edge are a number of shrubs, especially

poison sumac and spicebush. Blackberry, grape, red osier and witch hazel also can be spotted.

At 0.6 miles, the trail reaches the beginning of the first loop. Go right/northeast, staying on the loop's north side.

Though about 8000 years old, Cowles Bog during the past century has undergone major changes thanks to agriculture and industrialization. Prior to the 1960s, the bog was noticeably open but since has become increasingly wooded. Hybrid cattails also have replaced a diverse sedge meadow. In 2009, the National Park Service began to restore the bog. Orchids notably have returned to it.

The hike reaches the second loop at 1.1 miles from the trailhead. Rather than head into the dunes, go left/southwest.

This segment of the first loop runs through a black oak savanna, a mix of the Great Plains' prairies and the East's hardwood forests. As the black oak trees are spaced apart, sunlight bathes the open spaces, allowing for a number of meadow grasses and wildflowers to also flourish.

Interdunal ponds sit northwest of the savanna. You also may notice small hills rising on the horizon; these are forested dunes with Mount Bentley directly north and Mount Tuthill to the northwest. On the other side of the dunes is a Lake Michigan beach.

At 1.4 miles, the loop reaches a junction. Go left/southeast to stay on the first loop. You're now officially on the Greenbelt Trail.

The path heads back into Cowles Bog. Little Lake soon appears on the trail's left/north side. At about 1.7 miles, the trail curves away from the lake and heads along a strip of high ground between the Eastern Wetlands on the right/south and a pond on the left/north side.

A number of birds and insects make the bog their home. But

The Cowles Bog – which really is a fen – in spring. NPS photo.

white-tailed deer also find food and protection from predators there. In the past, beavers have moved into the surrounding wetlands.

At 1.95 miles, the path junctions with the first loop's east side. Turn left/northeast onto it. This puts you back on the Cowles Bog Trail.

Cowles Bog stretches across the horizon on the trail's right/east side. The bog was named for Henry Cowles, a University of Chicago botanist whose study of sand dunes here during the turn of the 19th to 20th centuries established him as North America's "father of plant ecology." The bog is the only remaining ecosystem of the "Central Dunes" that Cowles studied.

At 2.25 miles, the loop comes full circle. Go right/east onto the stem trail and retrace your steps back to the parking lot.

Insect repellent is an absolute must on this trail. As much of the route is unshaded, be sure to don sunscreen, sunglasses and sunhat. Also, given this is a wetlands, hiking boots with good traction are necessary.

Other Wetlands Trails

Among the most important features of Indiana Dunes National Park is its great number of wetlands. While previous generations considered them wastelands that needed to be drained off, today we recognize that marshes support a large number of plants and animals, improve water quality, and reduce erosion and flooding. All of this makes them an interesting place to explore and to learn about our environment.

Bogs, fens and interdunal ponds dot the national park. Among the best of them to discover via day trails are:

• **Great Marsh** – Sometimes the best way to appreciate a wetlands is from a vista, the marsh stretching like a miles-wide impressionist painting before you as a variety of birds congregate or swoop in for a meal. A good way to observe the vast Great Marsh this way is via the **Dune Ridge Trail**, a 0.7-mile lollipop trail near Beverly Shores, Ind. Pick up the trail at the parking lot off of East State Park Road north of U.S. Hwy. 12. In contrast, the 1.26-miles **Great Marsh Trail** lets hikers walk through the wetlands where they can several migratory birds – including sandhill cranes and great blue herons – each spring and autumn. The trail starts from the South Lot off of Broadway Avenue north of Hwy. 12.

• **Inland Marsh** – The 2.6-mile **Tolleston Dunes Trail** heads through the Inland Marsh near Ogden Dunes. While the high points on the trail run through an oak savanna, the areas of lower ground are wetlands. Park in the lot at the end of the entry road off of Hwy. 12, about 0.15 miles west of Hillcrest Road.

• **Interdunal wetlands** – Connecting Calumet Dunes Paved Trail and Glenwood Dunes Trail to the National Lakeshore's Dunewood Campground, the 4.4-miles round trip **Dunewood Trace Campground Trail** skirts wetlands south of the Great

Marsh. The water-filled depressions at the base of and between small dunes sits less than a mile from Lake Michigan. This is a good trail if heading from the campground or if looking to extend a walk along the Calumet or Glenwood trails.

• **Miller Woods** – The first two loops of the **Paul H. Douglas Trail** (formerly the Miller Woods Trail and now sometimes referred to as the **Douglas Center Loop**) wind around wetlands and an interdunal pond for a 0.9-mile hike. A boardwalk cuts across the pond to form the loops' shared leg. Park at the Douglas Center for Environmental Education off of North Lake Street north of Hwy. 12.

• **Pinhook Bog** – Two trails pass through the acidic swamp. The **Pinhook Bog Trail** runs 0.86-miles round trip (with 0.26 miles of restricted to ranger-led hikes) and features several unique plants, including five that are carnivorous. The **Pinhook Upland Trail** is a 2.1-mile round trip lollipop that cuts through a beech and maple forest while offering great views of the bog.

Historical Sites

Chellberg Farm Trail

Day hikers can visit a historic Midwest homestead from the 1800s on the Chellberg Farm Trail.

The 1.7-miles round trip described here is the northern segment of the rustic Bailly Homestead/Chellberg Farm Trail. A variety of other historical places – including the Bailly homestead and the Bailly cemetery – are nearby.

To reach the trailhead, from Chicago go east on U.S. Hwy. 12 or from Michigan City, Ind., head west on the same road. In the Porter, Ind., area, turn east onto Oak Hill Road/County Road 1350 N then right/south onto Howe Road. Park in the Mnoké Prairie lot across the road from the entry to the Indiana Dunes Environmental Learning Center.

The trail heads east from the lot. In 0.2 miles, you'll reach one of the many loops in the Baily/Chellberg Trails System. Go left/north onto the loop, which passes through a peaceful forest of maple, beech, basswood and oak trees.

During the mid-1800s until the Great Depression, this area of Indiana – known as Baillytown – attracted a number of Swedish immigrants who formed a close-knit community. Among them was the Kjellberg family (or Chellbergs, as they became known), who emigrated to the United States in 1863.

At 0.5 miles from the trailhead, the trail reaches a junction connecting to the Bailly Cemetery and the Little Calumet River Trail. Continue to the Chellberg Farm by going straight-right/east.

Just six years after arriving in America, the Kjellbergs bought the 80-acre property now known as the Chellberg Farm. They paid a mere $12 an acre.

The trail soon curves south then east again. In 0.8 miles from the trailhead, it reaches the historic Chellberg Farm.

The Chellburg family barn was built in the 1870s. NPS photo.

Several historic buildings can be explored on the homestead. Among the most popular of them is the farmhouse. Built in 1885, its folk Victorian style was common across the United States at the time. The red brick facade is made of porter brick, which was created from nearby clay.

The barn is slightly older than the farmhouse. Constructed sometime during the 1870s, it is nearly 51 feet long by 25 feet wide and 25 feet tall. A three-bay structure with gabled roof, several improvements were made to it over the years, including the addition of a silo in 1917 and a concrete floor in 1938.

Two other common farm buildings of the era that still exist on the site are the corncrib and the granary. The Kjellbergs over the generations used several types of corncribs; the one now standing was built in 1941. The granary is the two-story, wooden building west of the farmhouse.

Also on the property is a maple sugar camp set up in the 1930s that is still used today. Every year in early March, the national park hosts a Maple Sugar Time festival in which visitors can tap their own syrup. Indiana Dunes is the only national park that makes maple syrup.

After taking in the historic sights, retrace your steps to the parking lot.

Other Historical Sites Trails

Hikers can explore several historic sites – from pioneer homesteads to homes of the future – at Indiana Dunes.

Humans have lived in the Indiana Dunes area since about 13,000 B.C. when the last ice age's glaciers retreated from the area. Scattered artifacts have been found on the higher and older dune ridges. More recently, Native American villages existed in the area, but most signs of them disappeared as Euro-American settlers arrived in the area during the 1800s. Because of that, the park's historic sites focus on sites from the 19th and 20th centuries.

Among the historic sites that can be hiked in the park are:

• **Bailly Cemetery** – Hikers can visit a family and community cemetery dating to 1827 on a 1.9-mile round trip hike on the Bailly Homestead/Chellberg Farm Trail. The cemetery sits about a mile north of the Bailly Homestead on the edge of a sand ridge. Pioneer fur trader Joseph Bailly selected the sand hill to bury his son and erected a thirty-foot wooden cross near the grave. Soon, other members of the Swedish community buried their deceased there. Park at the Chellberg Farm off of Mineral Springs Road south of U.S. Hwy. 12 and head north on the trail for a 1-mile round trip.

• **Bailly Homestead** – After running his fur-trading post on the Little Calumet River, Joseph Bailly established this farm in the early 1830s when the U.S. government opened northern Indiana to settlement. Among the buildings remaining is the Bailly House (construction began in 1834), a chapel that was a summer kitchen, a log house that was the Bailly's dairy house and tool shed built in the mid-1870s, and a brick house from 1874. Park in the lot off of Howe Road south of Oak Hill Road and head south on the trail for a 0.7-mile round trip.

• **1933 Century of Progress World's Fair homes of the future** – You can hike back to the future in a ranger-led tour of five historic homes erected during the 1933 Chicago World's Fair to show what homes of the future would look like. Throughout a single day each October, two-hour walking tours are given of the Cypress Log Cabin, the House of Tomorrow, Florida Tropical, Armco Ferro, and the Wieboldt-Rostone houses. While some of the predictions, such as central air conditioning and dishwashers, came true, others – like the house with an airplane hangar on the first floor (after all, everyone in the future would have an airplane) – proved less than prophetic. In 1935, a developer brought the houses to the dunes hoping to attract home buyers to his resort community of Beverly Shores. Each of the homes are on the National Register of Historic Places.

• **Good Fellow Youth Camp** – U.S. Steel operated a summer camp for its employees' children for more than three decades in the mid-20th century. Every week for two months, between 60-100 kids aged 8-15 enjoyed outdoors activities at the camp in a forest near Lake Michigan. No formal trail runs through the grounds, but you still can follow road sides and walk around the camp's nine buildings and a swimming pool that remain on a 0.5-mile trek. Park at the Dunes Learning Center off of County Road 150 West/Howe Road south of County Road 1350 North/West Oak Hill Road.

Meandering Rivers
Little Calumet River Trail

Day hikers can explore a meandering river on the Little River Calumet Trail.

The 3.1-miles round trip trail forms a loop that crosses the Little Calumet River twice. For portions of the walk, the trail also briefly heads alongside the river and a wetlands bordering the waterway. It is part of the Bailly/Chellberg Trails System.

To reach the trailhead, from Chicago go east on U.S. Hwy. 12 or from Michigan City, Ind., head west on the same road. In the Porter, Ind., area, turn east onto Oak Hill Road/County Road 1350 N then right/south onto Howe Road. After crossing and running alongside the Little Calumet River for about a fifth of the mile, the road forks; go right/southwest and park in the lot when the road runs out. From the lot, go left/west on the trail.

On the trail's left/south side is the recently restored Mnoké Prairie, which gives a glimpse of what the grasslands covering this part of the continent looked like when Euro-American settlers arrived in the 1800s. Farmed for decades, the park service has restored the 120-acre site to its prairie state, even performing prescribed burns to mimic the natural fires necessary to the cycle of plant life in that ecosystem.

At 0.9 miles from the trailhead, the route curls north with a bridge crossing the Little Calumet River. Also known as the East Arm Little Calumet River or the Little Calumet River East Branch, this stretch is one of the few undisturbed portions of the 22.1-mile long waterway.

Before 1926, the stream connected to the Little Calumet River in Illinois, but that year construction of the Burns Waterway diverted the route so it drained into Lake Michigan at Burns Harbor in Indiana.

The river meanders here thanks to the easily erodible soil,

The Little Calumet River in the park used to run all the way to Chicago. NPS photo.

which once the sandy bottom of Glacial Lake Chicago that covered this section of Indiana and the bottom third of modern Lake Michigan about 14,000 years ago. As a bend forms in a river, the river erodes sediment from the outer curve and deposits it on an inner curve further downstream. The result is that the meanders grow larger and larger over time so that the river shifts from somewhat straight to coiled in appearance.

North of the bridge, the trail enters a marsh on the river's north side and becomes a boardwalk.

Along much of the waterway, farm fields ran right up to its edge. Without the riparian vegetation, field run-off carried sediment and fertilizer straight into the river. The result was reduced water quality and clarity.

As the trail leaves the marsh, it curls east and enters a mature hardwood forest of maple, beech, basswood and oak. During September, this is a perfect stretch to see autumn leaves, as yellows, orange and both deep and bright reds light up the tree canopy and trail.

At 1.9 miles, the trail reaches Howe Road; carefully cross it. The trail continues through the forest.

A variety of wildlife call the forest and river marshes home. Look for tracks of white-tailed deer and coyote in the trail dirt. You're also certain to see and hear at least a few of the 352 species of birds. If visiting during late May to mid-June or mid-July to mid-August, you may spot the federally endangered Karner blue butterfly hovering near lupine.

At 2.1 miles, you'll reach the first of several junctions in the woods that can be confusing and send you off in the wrong direction. First, go right/south. Then 0.1 miles later, go right/southwest at the next junction. The 2.5 miles mark passes a trail that leads to a parking lot; ignore that turn and continue left/south. Lastly, at 2.8 miles, turn right/southwest.

You'll soon pass the historic Bailly Homestead. In 1822, Honore Gratien Joseph Bailly de Messein established a fur trading post where several Native American trails converged at the Little Calumet River. He was one of the earliest Euro-American settlers in northern Indiana. The buildings here are all that remain of his homestead.

Continuing from the homestead, the trail reaches Howe Road again. Initially the trail parallels the road and then crosses the Little Calumet River.

You'll walk alongside the river for about 0.15 miles. You may spot kayakers plying the waters in this stretch. The river from here east past Chesterton, Ind., recently reopened to paddlers thanks to a gargantuan effort to remove log jams in the water. Kayakers had not be able to enjoy the waterway for three decades.

The hiking trail next turns away from the river and in 0.1 miles reaches your parking lot.

This hike absolutely requires insect repellent, especially in summer. After rain, the trail can be muddy, so be sure to wear hiking boots with good traction.

Other Waterway Trails

Only one river flows through Indiana Dunes National Park, but a couple of streams do make their way across the park, one as a tributary to the East Arm Little Calumet River and the other flowing directly into Lake Michigan:

• **Dunes Creek** – The 4.3-mile stream drains the Great Marsh and then West Branch (which drains Cowles Bog), passes through coastal sand dunes, and flows into Lake Michigan at Indiana Dunes State Park. Good trails to experience the creek are the **Calumet Bike Trail** (between Tremont Road and East State Park Boundary Road) and **Trail 2** in the state park.

• **Salt Creek** – This 24-mile tributary of the East Arm Little Calumet River flows north from Valparaiso, Ind. The Indiana Department of Natural Resources regularly stocks the creek with steelhead trout, Chinook salmon, and coho salmon. No park trails cross Salt Creek, but both the **Iron Horse Heritage** and the **Prairie Duneland** trails just south of the park do.

Beaches

Portage Lakefront & Riverwalk

Ah, the beach – sunbathing and swimming, flying kites and building sand castles, enjoying a summer sunset or taking in the dramatic approach of a storm. All of that and more is possible for those visiting West Beach via the Portage Lakefront and Riverwalk.

A 0.9-mile loop allows hikers to explore the beaches, dunes and a waterfront at the facility. A fishing pier and 900-foot breakwater leading to a lighthouse can be added to the walk as well.

To reach the Portage Lakefront and Riverwalk, from Chicago head east on U.S. Hwy. 12 or from Portage, Ind., go north to the highway. Then take Hillcrest Road north and turn right/east onto Midwest Steele. At the roundabout, go right/east onto Riverwalk Drive. Park in the second lot, which is on the road's left/west side.

At the lot's northwest corner, walk north on the paved, wheelchair accessible trail. You'll pass some small, reclaimed dunes on a brownfield reclamation site. Believe it or not, as recently as 2008, this was the site of a steel corporation's settling ponds for industrial byproduct and a sewage treatment facility.

Today, the dune habitat and Lake Michigan beach is a major stopover for migrating birds. Throughout the summer, you'll spot surfers challenging the waves while others catch a tan on the beach sand. In winter, shelf ice forms along the beach's edge, attracting sightseers.

You can swim Lake Michigan even when no lifeguards are on duty but be aware that rip currents and waves can make the water hazardous. You also can cook on the beach but must use one of the provided grills at a picnic shelter or an approved carry-in grill (which must have a noncombustible container

The pavilion on West Beach. NPS photo.

with an enclosed bottom and enclosed sides with a minimum depth of 2 inches); any charcoal has to be cooled and disposed of in a noncombustible container or taken when you leave. Glass containers cannot be used on the beach. Also, rocks and shells cannot be taken from the beach.

On the beach's east side is a 3,500 square foot public pavilion seasonal snack bar, restrooms, and a glass wall where migrating birds can be watched from the warmth of the indoors. There's also a breakwater that heads to a modern beacon light marking the Burns Waterway, which is the East Arm of the Little Calumet River. The lighthouse marking the entry's other side is a pretty sight.

The trail next curls past the pavilion and offers a spur to a fishing pier. With a permit, you can fish after hours.

Next the paved route heads north paralleling the waterway. Part of the trail is a wooden walkway along the river.

The trail crosses Riverwalk Drive to your parking lot. The

paved walkway also continues south to another lot.

The breakwater and riverwalk portion of the hike are closed from the last Monday of November through March 1 and at any other time if ice or snow are present.

Other Beach Trails

Indiana Dunes is a great destination for beach lovers. It features seven major beaches, listed here from west to east:

• **Miller Beach** – The Paul H. Douglas Trail (formerly the Miller Woods Trail) runs 2.1 miles (one-way) through forests to Miller Beach in Gary, Ind. While the Lake Michigan beach doesn't always offer the greatest views – industry sits on either side – it is the closest of the park's beach to Chicago and if hiking to reach it you get to cross incredibly high dunes, a fun adventure on its own. The trail starts at the Douglas Center for Environmental Education. Be aware that temperatures on the beach can be significantly colder or hotter than in the trail's wooded portion.

• **Long Lake Beach and West Beach** – Not all of the park's beaches sit on Lake Michigan. Loop 2 of the 1.2 miles-round trip West Beach Trail heads to a beach on Long Lake; it's a great spot for birding as well with a viewing platform for watching. If you prefer a beach on the Great Lake, however, no worries; just take the West Beach Trail to the 0.7-mile Dune Succession Trail (which is Loop 1 of the West Beach Trail) and follow it to a Lake Michigan shoreline perfect for sunbathing, building sand castles, or flying a kite. Pick up either trail at the parking lot off of West Beach Road east of County Line Road.

• **Porter Beach** – A quarter mile of Lake Michigan beachfront can be hiked near the park's center. Park in the lot at the end of Waverly Road north of U.S. Hwy. 20. The lot allows you to stroll the beach at neighboring Indiana Dunes State Park to

Porter Beach's east side. That stretch, if walking northeast, offers industry-free views on the horizon. The west end of Porter Beach also can be accessed via the Cowles Bog Trail, the third or westernmost loop of which runs 0.2 miles along Lake Michigan; you first have to pass a vast fen and major dunes, but the reward is an incredible amount of privacy on the beach.

• **Kemil Beach** – Immediately east of Indiana Dunes State Park, Kemil Beach offers far more than sands and waves. You can take a little time away from the beach umbrella and hike a dune or go birdwatching on the Dune Ridge Trail. A parking lot is off of East State Park Road north of U.S. Hwy. 12.

• **Dunbar Beach** – Immediately east of Kemil Beach, Dunbar is like going back to the future. In addition to swimming and suntanning, you can walk past five historic homes of tomorrow featured in the 1933 Century of Progress World's Fair. Park in the lot off of Lakeshore Drive east of East State Park Road.

• **Lake View** – While not much different from the adjacent Dunbar Beach, Lake View does offer covered picnic shelters that overlook Lake Michigan. Use the parking lot on Lakeshore Drive west of Broadway; do not park in the Town of Beverly Shores' private beach parking lot just east of the lot, though, as it's not part of the national park and can result in a ticket.

• **Central Beach** – This is one of the park's better beaches, as it's far from industry, unlike those on the park's west side. During spring and summer, bank swallows nest in the dunes. You can access the beach a couple of ways. One is to park at the end of Central Avenue north of U.S. Hwy. 12. For the more adventurous, instead take the Beach Trail, which leads to nearly a half-mile of Lake Michigan beachfront at the base of Mount Baldy Dune; the 1.12-miles round trip begins at the parking lot off of Rice Street north of U.S. Hwy. 12 just west of Michigan City, Ind.

Forest Wildlife
Tolleston Dunes Trail

Despite being smack dab in the middle of an urbanized area, there's plenty of wildlife to be seen at Indiana Dunes National Park. One good hike to spot them is the Tolleston Dunes Trail, which traverses a variety of ecosystems.

The 2.6-mile trail consists of a stem leading to two stacked loops. Though sporting a 127 feet gain in elevation, on average the grade is only 2 percent with a maximum grade of 9 percent.

To reach the trailhead, from Chicago head east on U.S. Hwy. 12 and from Portage, Ind., head north to that highway. Look for the entry road to the trail's parking lot about 0.15 miles west of Hillcrest Road, near Ogden Dunes. The lot sits on a former sand mining operation with the trail leaving from the southwest corner.

In 0.3 miles, the trail reaches rolling sand dunes. They were formed 4700 years ago when Lake Michigan's water level was about 25 feet higher and so reached this far inland.

Quite a range of animals make Indiana Dunes National Park their home, and many can be found at Tolleston Dunes. Among them are cottontail rabbits, garter snakes, opossums, raccoons, red fox, squirrels and white-tailed deer. Look to the sky, and you're likely to see great blue herons, hawks, mallards, turkey vultures, and a variety of songbirds.

You'll reach the first loop at 0.4 miles from the trailhead. Go right/northwest. The trail enters an oak savannah on the higher ground punctuated with wetlands at the low points. A boardwalk crosses one section of the wetlands.

In all, 41 different species of mammals, 352 birds species, 23 reptiles, and 18 species of amphibians can be found in the park. In the rivers and Lake Michigan, 71 kinds of fish make their home.

Butterflies along the Tolleston Dunes Trail. NPS photo.

Some of the park animals are quite rare. Among them are the federally threatened and endangered Indiana bat, the Eastern massasauga rattlesnake, the Rufa Red knot, and the Piping plover.

At 0.8 miles in, you'll reach the junction with the second loop. Go right/southwest onto the new loop.

Before Euro-Americans farmed and urbanized the area, a greater variety of wildlife could be found in the area. Elk, black bears and cougars all disappeared before the Civil War, while the gray wolf, river otter and porcupine vanished before World War I began.

After 1.8 miles from the trailhead, you'll reach the first loop. Go right/southeast onto it.

If you don't spot wildlife other than birds on the trail, they're probably just laying low. Most animals are active at dawn and dusk. Watch for their tracks, though, especially in sandy areas, which will let you know that one was nearby probably during the past day or so.

You'll reach the stem trail at 2.2 miles. Go right/northeast onto it and retrace your steps back to the parking lot.

If looking for a shorter version of the hike, skip the second loop and take the cut-off trail. This axes a mile off the hike for a 1.8-mile walk.

Tolleston Overlook

A quarter mile east of the parking lot entry road is a short boardwalk that heads to two overlooks. The elevated platforms give a great view of the wetlands and a dune ridge that the Tolleston Dune Trail winds through. In addition to being wheelchair accessible, shaded picnic tables can be found at the overlooks.

Other Wildlife Trails

Despite sitting in a built-up area at the edge of the nation's third largest urban area, there's plenty of wildlife to be seen at Indiana Dunes.

Two other trails that particularly stand out for spotting wildlife is:

• **Little Calumet River Trail** – Wildlife can be found across the river marshes and forest crossed by this 3.1-miles round trip trail. More than 350 species of birds can be spotted on the trail throughout the year. Also watch for whitetail deer and coyote tracks. From late-May through mid-August, the federally endangered Karner blue butterfly can be spotted near lupine. Park in the lot off of Howe Road south of Oak Hill Road/County Road 1350 N.

• **Paul H. Douglas Trail** – The 3.2-miles trail (formerly the Miller Woods Trail) passes a wetlands, oak savanna, and towering sand dunes, then ends at a Lake Michigan beach. Among the animals that can be seen along the trail are beaver, cottontail rabbit, coyote, eastern mole, fox squirrel, gray squirrel, long-tailed weasel, masked shrew, meadow vole, muskrat, prairie deer mouse, raccoon, red squirrel, short-tailed shrew, thirteen-lined ground squirrel, Virginia opossum, white-footed mouse, and white-tailed deer. Park at the Douglas Center for Environmental Education off of North Lake Street north of U.S. Hwy. 12.

• Also see the **Majestic Birds** section.

Diverse Flora

Pinhook Upland Trail

Boasting more than 1400 native plants, Indiana Dunes is among the National Park Service's most diverse sites for flora. A great way to see many of those plants – including some of the more exotic ones – is the Pinhook Upland Trail.

The 2.1-mile round trip lollipop trail cuts through a beech and maple forest while offering a great view of the Pinhook Bog.

To reach the trailhead, from Chicago take Interstate 94 east. In Michigan City, Ind., go south on U.S. Hwy 421 then head left/east onto Snyder Road/W 200 N. Next, go right/south onto North Wozniak Road. In a little more than a mile, turn left/east into the Pinhook Bog parking lot. This section of the national park is not part of its main units along the Lake Michigan shore.

From the lot, go east on the stem trail. The trail surface is packed dirt but can be slippery and muddy after a rain, so be sure to wear hiking boots with good traction.

The subtle changes in elevation so near Lake Michigan result in a variety of ecosystems, which in turn leads to a diversity of plant species throughout the park. Beaches and dunes, wetlands such as marshes and fens, oak savannas and wetland prairies, and hardwood forests, all can be found within the park.

Forests and a bog dominate the stem portion of the trail. At 0.3 miles in, the trail reaches the loop; go left/northeast onto it.

At a higher elevation than the bog, thus part of the loop runs through hardwood forests. Mature beech and maples shade a moraine, a ridge of sediment that was left by the edge of a glacier as it retreated about 15,000 years ago during the last ice age.

Just as the upland forest owes its existence to the area's

glacial history, so does the bog here. A chunk of the melting glacier left behind as the main one retreated depressed the land, forming a kettle lake. When the trapped glacier chunk fully melted, it filled the hole with water while pulverized clay and rock stuck inside it settled on the lake bottom.

The clay prevented the lake water from reaching groundwater or from springs and streams feeding the waterbody. As a result, this trapped meltwater grew increasingly stagnant and acidic over time.

At 0.7 miles, the trail reaches a 33-foot bridge with the bog on the trails' right/west side. Look for the light-green sphagnum moss covering the wetlands.

Sphagnum moss, which tolerates acidic water, forms floating mats over the lake. This in turn supports ferns, orchids (like pink lady's slipper), and even strange carnivorous plants such as pitcher plants and sundew. As parts of the bog fill in, blueberry and holly shrubs can take hold, which in turn opens the way for tamarack and red maple trees to take root.

The 38-foot bridge over the bog, at 0.9 miles from the trailhead, allow hikers to see these plants and many more.

The light-green mats of stringy sphagnum moss stand out in the bog and are even visible from the air. Thanks to compounds in the sphagnum's cell walls, the moss does not decay easily, trapping water. Be careful to not step on the solid-looking moss – in addition to potentially harming other rare plants that grow atop it, the mats can't fully support your weight, and you're sure to get wet.

That's true even of sphagnum moss that thickens up to six feet deep. If you spot blueberry and holly shrubs growing atop the moss, the mats are the deepest there.

At 1.2 miles in, the trail leaves the uplands for good and reaches a 53-foot bridge over the moss.

Secluded wetland on the Pinhook Upland Trail. NPS photo.

The Pinhook Bog stretches for 580 acres on both sides of the trail; sphagnum moss covers about a quarter of that area.

Breaking up the bog's many green hues are a number of flowers, most notably the pink lady's slipper. The only lady's slipper to lack stem leaves, it can grow up to 18 inches high. Other orchids here are the rose pogonia, which usually can be seen near the end of boardwalks, and the yellow fringed orchid.

Five carnivorous plants make the bog their home. The tiny spoonleaf sundew has spoon/teardrop-shaped leaves covered in mucilage-tipped tentacles that ensnare insects. Round-leaved sundew also has flypaper-styled leaves, which are round rather than teardrop-shaped. The purple pitcher plant's leaves curl into a pitcher or cup half-filled with water and juices that trap and digest bugs. Hidden-fruited bladderwort feeds on small aquatic insects it captures in a bladder-shaped trap while the horned bladderwort does the same to small insects atop the soil.

At 1.7 miles, the loop reaches the stem trail. Go left/northwest onto it and retrace your steps back to parking lot.

Insect repellent is a must on this trail. Also, beware of poison sumac, which grows on the bog's outer edges, known as the "moat"; poison sumac has compound leaves of seven to thirteen pointed leaflets with smooth edges.

Other Diverse Flora Trails

Hikers can see a whole variety of flora at Indiana Dunes, which is among the most biologically diverse units in the national park system. Fens, foredunes, riversides and hardwood forests all provide different habitats for often unique plants. Indeed, Indiana Dunes boasts more than 370 species of flowering plants with thirteen of them threatened or in danger of extinction.

Among the park's best trails to see interesting flora are:

• **Cowles Bog Trail** – Day hikers can see what plants conspire to make a fen such a frightening place on this 2.85-miles round trip trail. While red maple and yellow birch rule the uplands edging Cowles Bog, the swamp is covered in tamarack growing out of partially decomposed plants settling into a mire. Along the bog's edge are poison sumac, spicebush, blackberry, grape, red osier and witch hazel. Park in the lot off of N. Mineral Springs Road north of U.S. Hwy. 12.

• **Dune Ridge Trail** – A variety of habitats along this 0.7-mile loop trail ensure you'll see a range of interesting plants that thrive on sand dunes. The foredunes section of the trail boasts marram, little bluestem grasses, and cottonwoods. Marram is particularly adapted to living in moving dunes, but they succumb to taller plants' shade. This layer of dead grass provides the soil needed for the oak savanna that replaces it. The trail leaves from the lot on East State Park Road north of Hwy. 12.

• **Heron Rookery Trail** – Every spring, wildflowers cover the forest floor along the East Arm Little Calumet River on this 3.3-miles round trip trail. Trillium, Dutchman's breeches, and spring beauties are among only a few of the flowers that bloom before tree leaves unfurl. The trail offers the national park's most extensive display of spring wildflowers. Start at the parking lot off of 600 East south of 1350 North.

• **Paul H. Douglas Trail** – At least 287 species of plants and animals make their home in the Miller Woods, which this 3.2-miles trail (formerly the Miller Woods Trail) crosses. Among the interesting plants is the federally threatened Pitcher's thistle. The fame flower also roots here but nowhere else in the park. The woods boasts colorful wildflower blooms, especially of columbine and trailing arbutus. Start the hike at the Douglas Center for Environmental Education on North Lake Street north of Hwy. 12.

• **Pinhook Bog Trail** – Among the best spots to see exotic plants in the park is this 0.86-mile trail, which runs through a depression within a moraine. You'll see five carnivorous plants: the tiny spoonleaf sundew; round-leaved sundew; purple pitcher plant; hidden-fruited bladderwort; and horned bladderwort. While the neighboring Pinhook Upland Trail is open at all times, the bog only can be accessed on ranger-led tours. The trailhead is off North Wozniak Road south of Snyder Road/W 200 N.

• **Tolleston Dune Trail** – This 2.6-mile trail is well-known for its wildlife, but what attracts so many animals is the great diversity of plant life here. A rare black oak savanna covers the dunes, providing food and homes to a number of mammals. The leaves of the wild blue lupine flower, which grows abundantly here, provides meals for the caterpillar of the Karner blue butterfly, a federally endangered species. The trail leaves from the lot off of Hwy. 12 west of Hillcrest Road.

• **West Beach Trail** – Hikers can spot an Arizona beauty – eastern prickly pear cactus – in Indiana on this 1.2 miles-round trip trail, which heads to a beach on Long Lake. The cactus's fruit and pads provide dinner for coyote, gray fox, cottontail rabbits, striped skunks, and white-tailed deer while its flowers offer nectar and pollen to a variety of bees. Pick up the trail at the parking lot off of West Beach Road east of County Line Road.

Restored Prairies
Prairie Marsh and Savanna Trails

Not all of Indiana Dunes National Park is sand dunes, bogs and beachfront. A good portion of it also preserves prairieland. A great way to explore this fascinating ecosystem is the Prairie Marsh and Savanna trails, located at the park's Hoosier Prairie Nature Preserve.

The 0.8-mile hike consists of a stem and two connected loops in a 1547-acre area being restored and protected by a variety of agencies from the U.S. and Indiana governments to private nature preservation organizations. It's located a few miles south of the main park.

To reach the trailhead, from Chicago take either Interstate 90 or Interstate 94 east. Go right/south onto Indiana 912, which becomes Cline Avenue. The road ends at Main Street in Griffith, Ind. Go right/west onto Main Street. In a little more than a mile, look for a parking lot on the street's left/south side; if you've crossed Kennedy Avenue, you've gone too far. The stem trail heads south from the lot's east side.

The hike begins by crossing prairie that is part of the original land a nature conservancy purchased in 1970. Their goal was to save some of the last few acres of prairie as the pioneers would have seen much of this part of the state when they arrived in the early 1800s.

In about 0.05 miles, you can take a very short spur to the right/west. The 30 acres before you was a wheat field when purchased and added to the protected prairie in 1974. With very little assistance from man, the field over the decades has largely returned to its natural prairie state. Asters, big bluestem prairie grass, goldenrods, rattlesnake master, and tall coreopsis dominate the landscape with bobolink, goldfinch, meadowlarks, sparrows calling it home.

The stem reaches the first loop, the Prairie Marsh Trail, at 0.1 miles. Turn left/west onto it. The route enters true virgin prairie.

It's a good mix of dry and mesic prairies. The dry prairies, found on the higher ground, are reminiscent of those to the west on the Great Plains. Mesic prairies are on the lower ground, which usually has wetter soil and is typical of what grows in central Indiana and Illinois. Note how the plants of the two prairie types differ with just a few feet of elevation change.

After the trail curves south, a connector trail heads left/east. Go onto it, and at the next junction, you'll reach the second loop, or the Savanna Trail. Take it clockwise by going left/northeast.

If hiking on a warm summer day, you may notice a pleasant scent in the air. It comes from sweetfern, which grows along this stretch of the loop. It and the bracken found here are rare prairie plants in Indiana.

The trail soon enters an oak savanna, a prairie in which trees grow widely apart. In this part of Indiana, black and white oaks are most common in savannas.

Although those two oaks prospered here thanks to their ability to resist drought, a common condition in prairies, their hardiness proved their undoing. Settlers thirsting for wood cut almost all of the oaks during the 1800s. Today, oak savannas – once Indiana's dominant type of prairie – are now rarer in the state than are grasslands.

As the loop reaches its southeast side, beyond the small oak trees is a small marsh, known as a wet prairie. Sedges grow in the water, but also can see prairie cordgrass and bluejoint grass here. Several wildflowers also can be spotted, including grass pink orchid, marsh blazing star, marsh phlox, and prairie

Hoosier Prairie includes an oak savanna. NPS photo.

sundrops.

The next trail junction is with the connector to the Prairie Marsh Trail. Go left/west onto the connector, then at the next intersection take a left/south onto the Prairie Marsh.

On the south side of that loop, the trail passes another prairie marsh. In contrast to cattail-dominated wetlands found across much of the Midwest, this marsh enjoys a wide variety of flora. That helps make it a haven for a variety of salamanders, birds, reptiles and insects. Of all the prairie types crossed on the trail, you're most likely to see wild animals here.

Other animals you'll spot on the trail include white-tailed deer, red fox, minks, woodchucks, and eastern chipmunks. Red-tailed hawks often circle overhead, looking for a meal of white-footed mice or meadow voles. Yellowthroats, song sparrows, and swamp sparrows can be heard singing.

At the next two trail junctions, continue straight/north. You're back on the stem trail that goes to the parking lot.

Other Prairie Trails

Prior to the arrival of settlers from the East Coast and Europe, about 1 in every 7 acres of Indiana was prairieland. Agriculture, drainage and urbanization quickly decimated the prairies, and by the end of the 20th century, only a few pristine remnants remained. Fortunately, some of those parcels – as well as new efforts at restoring prairie – can be found at the national park.

Two other prairies that day trails explore at the park include:

• **Mnoké Prairie** – Indiana sits in a zone where the Eastern forests give way to the grassy Great Plains of the West. While oak savannas made up much of the area's meadows in that transition, swaths of tallgrass prairie did exist in the Hoosier State. Most were converted to farmland once settlers arrived. Recently, a tallgrass prairie was restored near the historic Bailly and Chellberg farm. You can walk the edge of it on the first segment of the **Little Calumet River Trail**; park in the lot at the end of of Howe Road south of Oak Hill Road and head west on the trail until coming the river bridge for a 1.8-mile round trip.

• **Dune Ridge black oak savanna** – Before Euro-American settlers arrived, black oak savannas were among the Midwest's most common ecosystems. Today, less than .02% of oak savanna remains. They still can be seen at Indiana Dunes, though; one great route for walking through them is the 0.7-mile **Dune Ridge Trail**, a lollipop trail near Beverly Shores, Ind. Pick up the trail at the parking lot off of East State Park Road north of U.S. Hwy. 12.

Nearby Trails

Despite being urbanized, the area around Indiana Dunes National Park boasts a variety of great beaches, municipal or county parks, and other lengthy hiking trails. These trails often allow you to escape the national park's summer beach crowds while experiencing local life.

Haunted Dunes

Nature Center Trail
Indiana Dunes State Park

The otherworldly, massive dunes in Indiana constantly shift and ripple about as if an apparition, but the next ghost-like form you see there may not be a sand but the spirit of a murdered woman.

Believers in the supernatural say the spirit of Alice Marble Gray, a daughter of one of Chicago's most powerful families, makes her home at Indiana Dunes State Park along the Lake Michigan shore. A 1.25-mile foray into the park allows you to enjoy the beautiful dunes – and provides an opportunity to experience the scare of your life.

To reach the dunes, from Interstate 94 take the Indiana Hwy. 49 exit in Chesterton, Ind. Head north on Hwy. 49 into the park. After passing the park office, turn right. At the next junction, go right once more. Drive past three more road junctions until coming to the North Picnic Area. At the fourth junction, turn left, parking at the nature center.

The trailhead for the Nature Center Trail is on the parking lot's east side. Heading in that direction, you'll soon reach the sand dunes, which line three miles of spectacular beaches along Lake Michigan's southern shore. Sand dunes here can rise as high as 200 feet.

The Nature Center Trail serves as the stem for a lollipop trail through the dunes. Go counterclockwise on the trail. This places you on Trail 10 as you pass a marsh. Lake Michigan is to your left beyond the dune field.

During the 1910s, local fisherman began telling the tale of Diana of the Dunes, so named because they often reported a naked woman with the body of a Greek goddess frolicking about on the dunes and swimming in the lake. One man invest-

Lake Michigan beach and dunes at Indiana Dunes State Park.

igating the case soon discovered the woman was none other than Alice Marble Gray, who lived in a small lakeside cottage.

As the trail veers away from the marsh, Trail 10 breaks off and heads northeast, paralleling the lake. To make a loop, instead stay on the trail going north toward the lake.

Rather than rely on her family's fortunes, Alice worked several years as an editorial secretary for *Woman's World*. Upon amassing a little wealth, she moved to the lakeshore. Then, after five years of being alone, she met Paul Wilson, a drifter.

In 1922, the corpse of a brutally beaten man was found near their cottage, and police questioned them. They quickly moved away to get out of the public eye.

In about an eighth of a mile from where Trail 10 broke off, the loop intersects Trail 9. Go left/southwest, making the opposite side of the loop.

Three years later, Alice died – from complications arising

from repeated blows Wilson had landed upon her. Wilson fled with their children. He later was found in a California prison, but no one knows what became of their offspring.

Shortly after Alice's death, visitors to the dunes began seeing the ghost of a beautiful nude woman. Descriptions of her bear an uncanny resemblance to the young Diana of the Dunes who was so at peace with herself. Apparently Alice's spirit has gone to the one place where her mortal self experienced true happiness.

In about 0.4 miles, the loop junctions with the Nature Center Trail. Go right/west, returning to your vehicle.

Other Nearby Trails

Among your best bets for day trails outside of the national park are:

• **Indiana Dunes State Park** – The state park sits exactly in the middle of the national park on Lake Michigan's shores. Its 2182 acres offers many of the same features – beachfront, dunes, forests, wetlands, and prairie/savanna habitat – and so also attracts an incredible variety of birds. The mile-long **Trail 2** circles the Great Marsh on a boardwalk so you can keep your feet dry. Among the birds you can spot are: Baltimore oriole; bay-breasted, blackburnian, Canada, golden-winged, hooded, Kirtland's, and prairie warblers; blue jay; Louisiana waterthrush; scarlet tanager; and veery. A 3.5-mile round trip segment of **Trail 10** passes two blowouts – an exposed area where wind moved sand from the dunes through an area of plants. The park's two largest blowouts – Beach House and Furnessville – are on this segment, which starts at the Pavilion and Bathhouse.

• **Dune Nature Preserve** – Technically the eastern two-thirds of the state park, the preserve includes three dunes known as The Tremonts: Mt. Tom, which tops out a 192 feet above lake level; Mt. Holden, 184 feet; and Mt. Jackson, 176 feet. The 1.5-mile long **Trail 8** goes up and over each of the wooded Tremonts and runs from the Wilson Shelter to the Pavilion and Beach House.

• **Iron Horse Heritage Trail** – The 2.9-mile one-way gravel trail runs between Hamstrom Road and Indiana Hwy. 149/Max Mochal Road northeast of Portage, Ind. The best section is the eastern half, which runs along the edge of Portage Imagination County Park and a small lake.

• **Marquette Park** – A 1.4-mile white sand beach stretches along Lake Michigan at this Gary, Ind., park that is entirely sur-rounded by the national park. Formerly known as Lake Front Park, the area recently underwent a major $28 million over-haul. The beach is not a designated swimming area and is con-sidered an Important Bird Area. Park in the city lots at the end of North Lake Street north of U.S. Hwy. 12.

• **Oak Ridge Prairie and Savannah Trail** – The 9.5-mile one-way former railway turned asphalt trail runs from Erie Lackawanna Trail at South Arbogast Avenue in Griffith, Ind., to the Prairie Duneland Trail at Hobart Road in Hobart. The end points definitely are better than the center, which crosses busy Interstate 65 and Indiana Hwy. 53.

• **Oak Ridge Prairie County Park** – Several short trails run through this public area in the Lake County park system. Try the 0.56-mile Lake Perimeter Trail, which circles a pond through woodlands and an open green. Pick up the trail from the lot at the end of the park entry road east of South Colfax Street near Griffith, Ind.

• **Porter Brickyard Trail** – The paved 3.5-mile one-way trail runs north to south with one end in the national park (trailhead is at 1184 North Mineral Springs Road) and the other outside the park at 198 S. Jackson Blvd. in Chesterton, Ind. Along the way, it passes the Bailly-Chellberg historic sites and in Chesterton connects to the Prairie Duneland Trail.

- **Prairie Duneland Trail** – The 11.2-mile one-way trail links downtown Hobart, Ind., (trailhead is at 4 North Hobart Road) to a trailhead in Chesterton at 198 S. Jackson Blvd. The grade is nil, and there are six smaller parking lots along the trail route should you want to do a shorter walk.
- **Washington Park** – The Michigan City, Ind., city park boasts a 2-mile long Lake Michigan beach and a small zoo featuring 90 different species on a 15-acre campus. Park in the lot at the end of the Park Entrance Road north of Lake Shore Drive.

Bonus Section I: Day Hiking Primer

Y ou'll get more out of a day hike if you research it and plan ahead. It's not enough to just pull over to the side of the road and hit a trail that you've never been on and have no idea where it goes. In fact, doing so invites disaster.

Instead, you should preselect a trail (This book's trail descriptions can help you do that). You'll also want to ensure that you have the proper clothing, equipment, navigational tools, first-aid kit, food and water. Knowing the rules of the trail and potential dangers along the way also are helpful. In this special section, we'll look at each of these topics to ensure you're fully prepared.

Selecting a Trail

For your first few hikes, stick to short, well-known trails where you're likely to encounter others. Once you get a feel for hiking, your abilities, and your interests, expand to longer and more remote trails.

Always check to see what the weather will be like on the trail you plan to hike. While an adult might be able to withstand wind and a sprinkle here or there, for kids it can be pure misery. Dry, pleasantly warm days with limited wind always are best when hiking with children.

Don't choose a trail that is any longer than the least fit person in your group can hike. Adults in good shape can go 8-

12 miles a day; for kids, it's much less. There's no magical number.

When planning the hike, try to find a trail with a mid-point payoff – that is something you and definitely any children will find exciting about half-way through the hike. This will help keep up everyone's energy and enthusiasm during the journey.

If you have children in your hiking party, consider a couple of additional points when selecting a trail.

Until children enter their late teens, they need to stick to trails rather than going off-trail hiking, which is known as bushwhacking. Children too easily can get lost when off trail. They also can easily get scratched and cut up or stumble across poisonous plants and dangerous animals.

Generally, kids will prefer a circular route to one that requires hiking back the way you came. The return trip often feels anti-climatic, but you can overcome that by mentioning features that all of you might want to take a closer look at.

Once you select a trail, it's time to plan for your day hike. Doing so will save you a lot of grief – and potentially prevent an emergency. You are, after all, entering the wilds, a place where help may not be readily available.

When planning your hike, follow these steps:

• Print a road map showing how to reach the parking lot near the trailhead. Outline the route with a transparent yellow highlighter and write out the directions.

• Print a satellite photo of the parking area and the trailhead. Mark the trailhead on the photo.

• Print a topo map of the trail. Outline the trail with the yellow highlighter. Note interesting features you want to see along the trail and the destination.

• If carrying GPS, program this information into your device.

• Make a timeline for your trip, listing: when you will leave home; when you will arrive at the trailhead; your turn back time; when you will return for home in your vehicle; and when you will arrive at your home.

• Estimate how much water and food you will need to bring based on the amount of time you plan to spend on the trail and in your vehicle. You'll need at least two pints of water per person for every hour on the trail.

• Fill out two copies of a hiker's safety form. Leave one in your vehicle.

• Share all of this information with a responsible person remaining in civilization, leaving a hiker's safety form with them. If they do not hear from you within an hour of when you plan to leave the trail in your vehicle, they should contact authorities to report you as possibly lost.

Clothing
Footwear

If your feet hurt, the hike is over, so getting the right footwear is worth the time. Making sure the footwear fits before hitting the trail also is a good idea. With children, if you've gone a few weeks without hiking, that's plenty of time for feet to grow, and they may have just outgrown their hiking boots. Check out everyone's footwear a few days before heading out on the hike. If it doesn't fit, replace it.

For flat, smooth, dry trails, sneakers and cross-trainers are fine, but if you really want to head onto less traveled roads or tackle areas that aren't typically dry, you'll need hiking boots. Once you start doing any rocky or steep trails – and remember that a trail you consider moderately steep needs to be only half that angle for a child to consider it extremely steep – you'll want hiking boots, which offer rugged tread perfect for handling rough trails.

Socks

Socks serve two purposes: to wick sweat away from skin and to provide cushioning. Cotton socks aren't very good for hiking, except in extremely dry environments, because they retain moisture that can lead to blisters. Wool socks or liner socks work best. You'll want to look for three-season socks, also known as trekking socks. While a little thicker than summer socks, their extra cushioning generally prevents blisters. Also, make sure kids don't put on holey socks; that's just inviting blisters.

Layering

On all but hot, dry days, when hiking you should wear multiple layers of clothing that provide various levels of protection against sweat, heat loss, wind and potentially rain. Layering works because the type of clothing you select for each stratum serves a different function, such as wicking moisture or shielding against wind. In addition, trapped air between each layer of clothing is warmed by your body heat. Layers also can be added or taken off as needed.

Generally, you need three layers. Closest to your skin is the wicking layer, which pulls perspiration away from the body and into the next layer, where it evaporates. Exertion from walking means you will sweat and generate heat, even if the weather is cold. The second layer provides insulation, which helps keep you warm. The last layer is a water-resistant shell that protects you from rain, wind, snow and sleet.

As the seasons and weather change, so does the type of clothing you select for each layer. The first layer ought to be a loose-fitting T-shirt in summer, but in winter and on other cold days you might opt for a long-sleeved moisture-wicking synthetic material, like polypropylene. During winter, the next layer probably also should cover the neck, which often is exposed to the elements. A turtleneck works fine, but preferably not one made of cotton. The third layer in winter, depending on the temperature, could be a wool sweater, a half-zippered long sleeved fleece jacket, or a fleece vest.

You might even add a fourth layer of a hooded parka with pockets, made of material that can block wind and resist water. Gloves or mittens as well as a hat also are necessary on cold days.

Headgear

Half of all body heat is lost through the head, hence the hiker's adage, "If your hands are cold, wear a hat." In cool, wet weather, wearing a hat is at least good for avoiding hypothermia, a potentially deadly condition in which heat loss occurs faster than the body can generate it. Children are more susceptible to hypothermia than adults.

Especially during summer, a hat with a wide brim is useful in keeping the sun out of eyes. It's also nice should rain start falling.

For young children, get a hat with a chin strap. They like to play with their hats, which will fly off in a wind gust if not fastened some way to the child.

Sunglasses

Sunglasses are an absolute must if walking through open areas exposed to the sun and in winter when you can suffer from snow blindness. Look for 100% UV-protective shades, which provide the best screen.

Equipment

A couple of principles should guide your purchases. First,

the longer and more complex the hike, the more equipment you'll need. Secondly, your general goal is to go light. Since you're on a day hike, the amount of gear you'll need is a fraction of what backpackers shown in magazines and catalogues usually carry. Still, the inclination of most day hikers is to not carry enough equipment. For the lightness issue, most gear today is made with titanium and siliconized nylon, ensuring it is sturdy yet fairly light. While the following list of what you need may look long, it won't weigh much.

Backpacks

Sometimes called daypacks (for day hikes or for kids), backpacks are essential to carry all of the essentials you need – snacks, first-aid kit, extra clothing.

For day hiking, you'll want to get an internal frame, in which the frame giving the backpack its shape is inside the pack's fabric so it's not exposed to nature. Such frames usually are lightweight and comfortable. External frames have the frame outside the pack, so they are exposed to the elements. They are excellent for long hikes into the backcountry when you must carry heavy loads.

As kids get older, and especially after they've been hiking for a couple of years, they'll want a "real" backpack. Unfortunately, most backpacks for kids are overbuilt and too heavy. Even light ones that safely can hold up to 50 pounds are inane for most children.

When buying a daypack for your child, look for sternum straps, which help keep the strap on the shoulders. This is vital for prepubescent children, as they do not have the broad shoulders that come with adolescence, meaning packs likely will slip off and onto their arms, making them uncomfortable and difficult to carry. Don't buy a backpack that a child will "grow into." Backpacks that don't fit well simply will lead to sore shoulder and back muscles and could result in poor posture.

Also, consider purchasing a daypack with a hydration system for kids. This will help ensure they drink a lot of water. More on this later when we get to canteens.

Before hitting the trail, always check your children's backpacks to make sure that they have not overloaded them. Kids think they need more than they really do. They also tend to overestimate their own ability to carry stuff. Sibling rivalries often lead to children packing more than they should in their rucksacks, too. Don't let them overpack "to teach them a lesson," though, as it can damage bones and turn the hike into a bad experience.

A good rule of thumb is no more than 25 percent capacity. Most upper elementary school kids can carry only about 10 pounds for any short distance. Subtract the weight of the backpack, and that means only 4-5 pounds in the backpack. Overweight children will need to carry a little less than this or they'll quickly be out of breath.

Child carriers

You'll have to carry infant and toddlers. Until infants can hold their heads up, which usually doesn't happen until about four to six months of age, a front pack (like a Snugli or Baby Bjorn) is best. It keeps the infant close for warmth and balances out your backpack. At the same time, though, you must watch for baby overheating in a front pack, so you'll need to remove the infant from your body at rest stops.

Once children reach about 20 pounds, they typically can hold their heads up and sit on their own. At that point, you'll want a baby carrier (sometimes called a child carrier or baby backpack), which can transfer the infant's weight to your hips when you walk. You'll not only be comfortable, but your child will love it, too.

Look for a baby carrier that is sturdy yet lightweight. Your child is going to get heavier as time passes, so about the only way you can counteract this is to reduce the weight of the items you use to carry things. The carrier also should have adjustment points, as you don't want your child to outgrow the carrier too soon. A padded waist belt and padded shoulder straps are necessary for your comfort. The carrier should provide some kind of head and neck support if you're hauling an infant. It also should offer back support for children of all ages, and leg holes should be wide enough so there's no chafing. You want to be able to load your infant without help, so it should be stable enough to stand that way when you take it off the child can sit in it for a moment while you get turned around. Stay away from baby carriers with only shoulder straps, as you need the waist belt to help shift the child's weight to your hips for more comfortable walking.

Fanny packs

Also known as a belt bag, a fanny pack is virtually a must for anyone with a baby carrier, as you can't otherwise lug a backpack. If your significant other is with you, he or she can carry the backpack, of course. Still, the fanny pack also is a good alternative to a backpack in hot weather, as it will reduce back sweat.

If you have only one or two kids on a hike, or if they also are old enough to carry daypacks, your fanny pack need not be large. A mid-size pouch can carry at least 200 cubic inches of supplies, which is more than enough to accommodate all the materials you need. A good fanny pack also has a spot for hooking canteens to.

Canteens

Canteens or plastic bottles filled with water are vital for any hike, no matter how short the trail. You'll need to have enough of them to carry about two pints of water per person for every hour of hiking.

Trekking poles

Also known as walking poles or walking sticks, trekking poles are necessary for maintaining stability on uneven or wet surfaces and to help reduce fatigue. The latter makes them useful on even surfaces. By transferring weight to the arms, a trekking pole can reduce stress on your knees and lower back, allowing you to maintain a better posture and to go farther.

If an adult with a baby or toddler on your back, you'll primarily want a trekking pole to help you maintain your balance, even if on a flat surface, and to help absorb some of the impact of your step.

Graphite tips provide the best traction. A basket just above the tip is a good idea so the stick doesn't sink into mud or sand. Angled cork handles are ergonomic and help absorb sweat from your hands so they don't blister. A strap on the handle to wrap around your hand is useful so the stick doesn't slip out. Telescopic poles are a good idea as you can adjust them as needed based on the terrain you're hiking and as kids grow to accommodate their height.

The pole also needs to be sturdy enough to handle rugged terrain, as you don't want a pole that bends when you press it to the ground. Spring-loaded shock absorbers help when heading down a steep incline but aren't necessary. Indeed, for a short walk across flat terrain, the right length stick is about all you need.

Carabiners

Carabiners are metal loops, vaguely shaped like a D, with a sprung or screwed gate. You'll find that hooking a couple of them to your backpack or fanny pack useful in many ways. For example, if you need to dig through a fanny pack, you can hook the strap of your trekking pole to it. Your hat, camera straps, first-aid kit, and a number of other objects also can connect to them. Hook carabiners to your fanny pack or backpack upon purchasing them so you don't forget them when packing. Small carabiners with sprung gates are inexpensive, but they do have a limited life span of a couple of dozen hikes.

Navigational Tools

Paper maps

Paper maps may sound passé in this age of GPS, but you'll find the variety and breadth of view they offer to be useful. During the planning process, a paper map (even if viewing it online), will be far superior to a GPS device. On the hike, you'll also want a backup to GPS. Or like many casual hikers, you may not own GPS at all, which makes paper maps indispensable.

Standard road maps (which includes printed guides and handmade trail maps) show highways and locations of cities and parks. Maps included in guidebooks, printed guides handed out at parks, and those that are hand-drawn tend to be designed like road maps, and often carry the same positives and negatives.

Topographical maps give contour lines and other important details for crossing a landscape. You'll find them invaluable on a hike into the wilds. The contour lines' shape and their spacing on a topo map show the form and steepness of a hill or bluff, unlike the standard road map and most brochures and hand-drawn trail maps. You'll also know if you're in a woods, which is marked in green, or in a clearing, which is marked in white. If you get lost, figuring out where you are and how to get to where you need to be will be much easier with such information.

Aerial photos offer a view from above that is rendered exactly as it would look from an airplane. Thanks to Google and other online services, you can get fairly detailed pictures of the landscape. Such pictures are an excellent resource when researching a hiking trail. Unfortunately, those pictures don't label what a feature is or what it's called, as would a topo map. Unless there's a stream, determining if a feature is a valley bottom or a ridgeline also can be difficult. Like topo maps, satellite and aerial photos can be out of date a few years.

GPS

By using satellites, the global positioning system can find your spot on the Earth to within 10 feet. With a GPS device, you can preprogram the trailhead location and mark key turns and landmarks as well as the hike's end point. This mobile map is a powerful technological tool that almost certainly ensures you won't get lost – so long as you've correctly programmed the information. GPS also can calculate travel time and act as a compass, a barometer and altimeter, making such devices vir-tually obsolete on a hike.

In remote areas, however, reception is spotty at best for GPS, rendering your mobile map worthless. A GPS device also runs on batteries, and there's always a chance they will go dead. Or you may drop your device, breaking it in the process. Their screens are small, and sometimes you need a large paper map to get a good sense of the natural landmarks around you.

Compass

Like a paper map, a compass is indispensable even if you use GPS. Should your GPS no longer function, the compass then can be used to tell you which direction you're heading. A protractor compass is best for hiking. Beneath the compass needle is a transparent base with lines to help your orient yourself. The compass often serves as a magnifying glass to help you make out map details. Most protractor compasses also come with a lanyard for easy carrying.

Food and Water

Water

As water is the heaviest item you'll probably carry, there is a temptation to not take as much as one should. Don't skimp on the amount of water you bring, though; after all, it's the one supply your body most needs. It's always better to end up having more water than needed than returning to your vehicle dehydrated.

How much water should you take? Adults need at least a quart for every two hours hiking. Children need to drink about a quart every two hours of walking and more if the weather is hot or dry. To keep kids hydrated, have them drink at every rest stop.

Don't presume there will be drinking water on the hiking trail. Most trails outside of urban areas lack such an amenity. In addition, don't drink water from local streams, lakes, rivers or ponds. There's no way to tell if local water is safe or not. As soon as you have consumed half of your water supply, you should turn around for the vehicle.

Food

Among the many wonderful things about hiking is that

snacking between meals isn't frowned upon. Unless going on an all-day hike in which you'll picnic along the way, you want to keep everyone in your hiking party fed, especially as hunger can lead to lethargic and discontented children. It'll also keep young kids from snacking on the local flora or dirt. Before hitting the trail, you'll want to repackage as much of the food as possible as products sold at grocery stores tend to come in bulky packages that take up space and add a little weight to your backpack. Place the food in re-sealable plastic bags.

Bring a variety of small snacks for rest stops. You don't want kids filling up on snacks, but you do need them to maintain their energy levels if they're walking or to ensure they don't turn fussy if riding in a child carrier. Go for complex carbohydrates and proteins for maintaining energy. Good options include dried fruits, jerky, nuts, peanut butter, prepared energy bars, candy bars with a high protein content (nuts, peanut butter), crackers, raisins and trail mix (called "gorp"). A number of trail mix recipes are available online; you and your children may want to try them out at home to see which ones you collectively like most.

Salty treats rehydrate better than sweet treats do. Chocolate and other sweets are fine if they're not all that's served, but remember they also tend to lead to thirst and to make sticky messes. Whichever snacks you choose, don't experiment with food on the trail. Bring what you know kids will like.

Give the first snack within a half-hour of leaving the trailhead or you risk children becoming tired and whiny from low energy levels. If kids start asking for them every few steps even after having something to eat at the last rest stop, consider timing snacks to reaching a seeable landmark, such as, "We'll get out the trail mix when we reach that bend up ahead."

Milk for infants

If you have an infant or unweaned toddler with you, milk is as necessary as water. Children who only drink breastfed milk but don't have their mother on the hike require that you have breast-pumped milk in an insulated beverage container (such as a Thermos) that can keep it cool to avoid spoiling. Know how much the child drinks and at what frequency so you can bring enough. You'll also need to carry the child's bottle and feeding nipples. Bring enough extra water in your canteen so you can wash out the bottle after each feeding. A handkerchief can be used to dry bottles between feedings.

Don't forget the baby's pacifier. Make sure it has a string and hook attached so it connects to the baby's outfit and isn't lost.

What not to bring

Avoid soda and other caffeinated beverages, alcohol, and energy pills. The caffeine will dehydrate children as well as you. Alcohol has no place on the trail; you need your full faculties when making decisions and driving home. Energy pills essentially are a stimulant and like alcohol can lead to bad calls. If you're tired, get some sleep and hit the trail another day.

First-aid Kit

After water, this is the most essential item you can carry.

A first-aid kit should include:
- Adhesive bandages of various types and sizes, especially butterfly bandages (for younger kids, make sure they're colorful kid bandages)
- Aloe vera
- Anesthetic (such as Benzocaine)
- Antacid (tablets)

- Antibacterial (aka antibiotic) ointment (such as Neosporin or Bacitracin)
- Anti-diarrheal tablets (for adults only, as giving this to a child is controversial)
- Anti-itch cream or calamine lotion
- Antiseptics (such as hydrogen peroxide, iodine or Betadine, Mercuroclear, rubbing alcohol)
- Baking soda
- Breakable (or instant) ice packs
- Cotton swabs
- Disposable syringe (w/o needle)
- Epipen (if children or adults have allergies)
- Fingernail clippers (your multi-purpose tool might have this, and if so you can dispense with it)
- Gauze bandage
- Gauze compress pads (2x2 individually wrapped pad)
- Hand sanitizer (use this in place of soap)
- Liquid antihistamine (not Benadryl tablets, however, as children should take liquid not pills; be aware that liquid antihistamines may cause drowsiness)
- Medical tape
- Moisturizer containing an anti-inflammatory
- Mole skin
- Pain reliever (aka aspirin; for children's pain relief, use liquid acetaminophen such Tylenol or liquid ibuprofen; never give aspirin to a child under 12)
- Poison ivy cream (for treatment)
- Poison ivy soap
- Powdered sports drinks mix or electrolyte additives
- Sling
- Snakebite kit
- Thermometer

- Tweezers (your multi-purpose tool may have this allowing you to dispense with it)
- Water purification tablets

If infants are with you, be sure to also carry teething ointment (such as Orajel) and diaper rash treatment.

Many of the items should be taken out of their store packaging to make placement in your fanny pack or backpack easier. In addition, small amounts of some items – such as baking soda and cotton swabs – can be placed inside re-sealable plastic bags, since you won't need the whole amount purchased.

Make sure the first-aid items are in a waterproof container. A re-sealable plastic zipper bag is perfectly fine. As Indiana Dunes National Park sports a moist climate, be sure to re-place the adhesive bandages every couple of months, as they can deteriorate in the moistness. Also, check your first-aid kit every few trips and after any hike in which you've just used it, so that you can replace used components and to make sure medicines haven't expired.

If you have older elementary-age kids and teenagers who've been trained in first aid, giving them a kit to carry as well as yourself is a good idea. Should they find themselves lost or if you cannot get to them for a few moments, the kids might need to provide very basic first aid to one another.

Hiking with Children: Attitude Adjustment

To enjoy hiking with kids, you'll first have to adopt your child's perspective. Simply put, we must learn to hike on our kids' schedules – even though they may not know that's what we're doing.

Compared to adults, kids can't walk as far, they can't walk as fast, and they will grow bored more quickly. Every step we take requires three for them. In addition, early walkers, up to two years of age, prefer to wander than to "hike." Preschool kids will start to walk the trail, but at a rate of only about a mile per hour. With stops, that can turn a three-mile hike into a four-hour journey. Kids also won't be able to hike as steep of trails as you or handle as inclement of weather as you might.

This all may sound limiting, especially to long-time backpackers used to racking up miles or bagging peaks on their hikes, but it's really not. While you may have to put off some backcountry and mountain climbing trips for a while, it also opens to you a number of great short trails and nature hikes with spectacular sights that you may have otherwise skipped because they weren't challenging enough.

So sure, you'll have to make some compromises, but the payout is high. You're not personally on the hike to get a workout but to spend quality time with your children.

Family Dog

Dogs are part of the family, and if you have children, they'll want to share the hiking experience with their pets. In turn, dogs will have a blast on the trail, some larger dogs can be used as Sherpas, and others will defend against threatening animals.

But there is a downside to dogs. Many will chase animals and so run the risk of getting lost or injured. Also, a doggy bag will have to be carried for dog pooh – yeah, it's natural, but also inconsiderate to leave for other hikers to smell and for their kids to step in. In addition, most dogs almost always will lose a battle against a threatening animal, so there's a price to be paid for your safety.

Many places where you'll hike solve the dilemma for you as dogs aren't allowed on their trails. Dogs are verboten on some state and national parks trails but usually permitted on those in national forests. Always check with the park ranger before heading to the trail.

If you can bring a dog, make sure it is well behaved and friendly to others. You don't need your dog biting another hiker while unnecessarily defending the family.

Rules of the Trail

Ah, the woods or a wide open meadow, peaceful and quiet, not a single soul around for miles. Now you and your children can do whatever you want.

Not so fast.

Act like wild animals on a hike, and you'll destroy the very aspects of the wilds that make them so attractive. You're also likely to end up back in civilization, specifically an emergency room. And there are other people around. Just as you would wish them to treat you courteously, so you and your children should do the same for them.

Let's cover how to act civilized on the trail.

Minimize damage to your surroundings

When on the trail, follow the maxim of "Leave no trace." Obviously, you shouldn't toss litter on the ground, start rockslides, or pollute water supplies. How much is damage and how much is good-natured exploring is a gray area, of course. Most serious backpackers will say you should never pick up objects, break branches, throw rocks, pick flowers, and so on – the idea is not to disturb the environment at all.

Good luck getting a four-year-old to think like that. The good news is a four-year-old won't be able to throw around many rocks or break most branches.

Still, children from their first hike into the wilderness should be taught to respect nature and to not destroy their environment. While you might overlook a preschooler hurling rocks into a puddle, they can be taught to sniff rather than pick flowers. As they grow older, you can teach them the value of leaving the rock alone. Regardless of age, don't allow children to write on boulders or carve into trees.

Many hikers split over picking berries. To strictly abide by the "minimize damage" principle, you wouldn't pick any berries at all. Kids, however, are likely to find great pleasure in eating blackberries, currants and thimbleberries as ambling down the trail. Personally, I don't see any problem enjoying a few berries if the long-term payoff is a respect and love for nature. To minimize damage, teach them to only pick berries they can reach from the trail so they don't trample plants or deplete food supplies for animals. They also should only pick what they'll eat.

Collecting is another issue. In national and most state and county parks, taking rocks, flower blossoms and even pine cones is illegal. Picking flowers moves many species, especially if they are rare and native, one step closer to extinction. Archeological ruins are extremely fragile, and even touching them can damage a site.

But on many trails, especially gem trails, collecting is part of the adventure. Use common sense – if the point of the trail is to find materials to collect, such as a gem trail, take judiciously, meaning don't overcollect. Otherwise, leave it there.

Sometimes the trail crosses private land. If so, walking around fields, not through them, always is best or you could damage a farmer's crops.

Pack out what you pack in

Set the example as a parent: Don't litter yourself; whenever stopping, pick up whatever you've dropped; and always require kids to pick up after themselves when they litter. In the spirit of "Leave no trace," try to leave the trail cleaner than you found it, so if you come across litter that's safe to pick up, do so and bring it back to a trash bin in civilization. Given this, you may want to bring a plastic bag to carry out garbage.

Picking up litter doesn't just mean gum and candy wrappers but also some organic materials that take a long time to decompose and aren't likely to be part of the natural environment you're hiking. In particular, these include peanut shells, orange peelings, and eggshells.

Burying litter, by the way, isn't viable. Either animals or erosion soon will dig it up, leaving it scattered around the trail and woods.

Stay on the trail

Hiking off trail means potentially damaging fragile growth. Following this rule not only ensures you minimize damage but is also a matter of safety. Off trail is where kids most likely will encounter dangerous animals and poisonous plants. Not being able to see where they're stepping also increases the likelihood of falling and injuring themselves. Leaving the trail raises the chances of getting lost. Staying on the trail also means staying out of caves, mines or abandoned structures you may encounter. They are usually dangerous places.

Finally, never let children take a shortcut on a switchback trail. Besides putting them on steep ground upon which they could slip, their impatient act causes the switchback to erode.

Trail Dangers

On Indiana Dunes trails, two common dangers face hikers: ticks and poison ivy/sumac. Both can make miserable your time on the trail or once back home. Fortunately, both threats are easily avoidable and treatable.

Ticks

One of the greatest dangers comes from the smallest of creatures: ticks. Both the wood and the deer tick are common in Indiana Dunes and can infect people with Lyme disease.

Ticks usually leap onto people from the top of a grass blade as you brush against it, so walking in the middle of the trail away from high plants is a good idea. Wearing a hat, a long sleeve shirt tucked into pants, and pants tucked into shoes or socks, also will keep ticks off you, though this is not foolproof as they sometimes can hook onto clothing. A tightly woven cloth provides the best protection, however. Children can pick up a tick that has hitchhiked onto the family dog, so outfit Rover and Queenie with a tick-repelling collar.

After hiking into an area where ticks live, you'll want to examine your children's bodies (as well as your own) for them. Check warm, moist areas of the skin, such as under the arms, the groin and head hair. Wearing light-colored clothing helps make the tiny tick easier to spot.

To get rid of a tick that has bitten your child, drip either disinfectant or rubbing alcohol on the bug, so it will loosen its grip. Grip the tick close to its head, slowly pulling it away from the skin. This hopefully will prevent it from releasing saliva that spreads disease. Rather than kill the tick, keep it in a plastic bag so that medical professionals can analyze it should disease symptoms appear. Next, wash the bite area with soap and water then apply antiseptic.

In the days after leaving the woods, also check for signs of disease from ticks. Look for bulls-eye rings, a sign of a Lyme disease. Other symptoms include a large red rash, joint pain, and flu-like symptoms. Indications of Rocky Mountain spotted fever include headache, fever, severe muscle aches, and a spotty rash first on palms and feet soles that spread, all begin-ning about two days after the bite.

If any of these symptoms appear, seek medical attention immediately. Fortunately, antibiotics exist to cure most tick-related diseases.

Poison ivy/sumac

Often the greatest danger in the wilds isn't our own clumsiness or foolhardiness but various plants we encounter. The good news is that we mostly have to force the encounter with flora. Touching the leaves of either poison ivy or poison sumac in particular results in an itchy, painful rash. Each plant's sticky resin, which causes the reaction, clings to clothing and hair, so you may not have "touched" a leaf, but once your hand runs against the resin on shirt or jeans, you'll probably get the rash.

To avoid touching these plants, you'll need to be able to identify each one. Remember the "Leaves of three, let it be" rule for poison ivy. Besides groups of three leaflets, poison ivy has shiny green leaves that are red in spring and fall. Poison sumac's leaves are not toothed as are non-poisonous sumac, and in autumn their leaves turn scarlet. Be forewarned that even after leaves fall off, poison oak's stems can carry some of the itchy resin.

By staying on the trail and walking down its middle rather than the edges, you are unlikely to come into contact with this pair of irritating plants. That probably is the best preventative. Poison ivy barrier creams also can be helpful, but they only temporarily block the resin. This lulls you into a false sense of safety, and so you may not bother to watch for poison ivy.

To treat poison ivy/sumac, wash the part of the body that has touched the plant with poison ivy soap and cold water.

This will erode the oily resin, so it'll be easier to rinse off. If you don't have any of this special soap, plain soap sometimes will work if used within a half-hour of touching the plant. Apply a poison ivy cream and get medical attention immediately. Wearing gloves, remove any clothing (including shoes) that has touched the plants, washing them and the worn gloves right away.

For more about these topics and many others, pick up this author's "Hikes with Tykes: A Practical Guide to Day Hiking with Kids." You also can find tips online at the author's "Day Hiking Trails" blog at *hikeswithtykes.blogspot.com*. Have fun on the trail!

Bonus Section II:
National Parks Primer

T he breadth of wonders at America's national parks astounds the mind. You can stand at the nation's rooftop with 60 peaks taller than 12,000 feet at Rocky Mountain National Park or in a gash in the earth more than a mile deep at Grand Canyon. You can visit among the driest places in the world where little more than an inch of rain falls per year upon the beige sands of Death Valley or step into the blue ocean itself at Biscayne National Park where the bulk of the wilderness is the Atlantic and its vibrantly colored coral reefs. You can see some of the oldest rock on Earth, like the 1.2 billion year-old granite at Shenandoah National Park, to some of the newest land on the planet at Hawai'i Volcanoes National Park where you can watch lava flows create new ground inch by inch before you. You can enjoy parks that are primarily historical and even urban in nature, such as Cuyahoga Valley National Park, which features pioneer farms and bicycle paths, while others preserve breathless, awe-inspiring tracts of wild-erness and stone, such as Yosemite's El Capitan and Half Dome. You can trek through caves with rooms larger than a football field hundreds of feet below the ground, such as at Carlsbad Caverns, or beneath trees soaring 15 stories over your head at Redwood National Park.

Given these grand wonders, not surprisingly national parks are a major travel destination. Indeed, many parks report record attendance during past few years. In 2018, annual attendance at parks operated by the National Parks Service hit an amazing 338 million visits – the highest level ever in more than a century of record-keeping.

But with so many sights and given most national parks' distance from major population centers, how can visitors be sure they'll make the best use of their time and see all of the highlights?

Unfortunately, many park visitors treat a national park like a drive-through restaurant. Fully experiencing any national park, though, requires that you "get out of the car." As W.H. Davies once wrote, "Now shall I walk/Or shall I ride?/'Ride,' Pleasure said; 'Walk,' Joy replied." A day hike can deliver the joy that each park offers.

What is (and isn't) a national park

Often local tourism agencies and business groups will refer to the "national park" near their community. If you've done any amount of traveling, such statements on websites and brochures would lead you to believe that there are hundreds of national parks!

The truth of that matter is that many of those agencies and hometown boosters actually are referring to units administered by the National Park Service. The park service oversees more than 400 units, of which only 61 are actual national parks.

The types of units the park service manages are broken into more than 20 categories. Among the more common ones are national historical parks, national historic sites, national monuments, national memorials, national military parks, national battlefield parks, national battlefield sites, national battlefields, national preserves, and national reserves.

Other agencies also run parklands set aside for public use. The U.S. Forest Service overseas national forests. States and counties typically manage what are smaller versions of national parks and national forests. The U.S. Fish and Wildlife Service handles wildlife refuges while the Bureau of Land Management is in charge of wilderness areas.

As national forests and state parks adjoin national parks, travelers may not know when they've entered one unit or left another. Sometimes these different units even are operated as a single park, as is the case with the array of public lands protecting redwoods in northwestern California, to save costs.

National parks generally are considered the crown jewels of the park service's outdoor experiences. When visiting a national park, though, don't discount the surrounding state parks, national forests, and other recreational areas, as they also offer excellent sights to see. They're also often less crowded than a national park.

Choosing a park to visit

Planning a trip to a national park isn't like going to the mall. Unless you're lucky enough to live near a national park, any trip to one will be part of a vacation for you and your family. So you'll need to choose which park you want to visit.

Your interests

Begin by asking what you'd most like to see. Do you want to watch wildlife? Experience great geological features like canyons and exotic rock formations? Of deserts, volcanoes, autumn leaves, or tropical rain forests, which most appeals to you? Are you interested in history? Was there a park you've always wanted to visit since childhood?

The quandary you'll face is that you'll want to see more than you probably have vacation time for!

Getting there

Next, decide how you'll reach the park. Many parks are remote and require driving, at least from a nearby airport. How much time you have to travel and how much money you're able to spend on transportation can help you narrow your list of potential parks to visit during a vacation.

Costs

After that, determine how much money is in your budget. The good news is that the park itself is fairly inexpensive to visit. As of press time, Congaree National Park in South Carolina and Cuyahoga Valley National Park in Ohio are absolutely free to enter while at the upper end Grand Canyon National Park charges $30 a vehicle for a week-long stay.

Sometimes fees are reduced (and even waived) for students and military personnel. Generally, the vehicle pass you purchase is good for a few days.

Many times a year, the park service offers "free entrance days." Expect the park to be crowded on those days, however, as they often coincide with holidays.

If you plan to hike national parks regularly, you should consider purchasing a National Parks and Federal Recreational Lands Pass, which will get a noncommercial vehicle plus passholder and three passengers into any national park for less than $100 a year.

Even less expensive versions of the pass are available for senior citizens, the disabled and National Park volunteers. If you visit a number of parks over several weeks, you'll definitely save on admission costs going this route.

Be forewarned that there may be additional fees if planning

to camp or to park an RV. Almost any hike that involves being part of a tour group at a major destination within a park carries a cost beyond the entry fee.

The real cost will come in lodging and food. Hotels within national parks generally are pricey while those near the park entrances only slight less so. Camping in the park or a neighboring national forest can be a good, inexpensive option. Food also can cost a small fortune within a park, but usually there are plenty of good, less expensive alternatives in nearby communities.

When to visit

Another consideration is when you will travel. Parts of some parks, such as Rocky Mountain, Crater Lake and Yosemite, actually cannot be reached during winter as heavy snowfall closes high mountain roads. Others, such as Death Valley, are simply too dangerous to hike in the summer heat. Most parks also have a peak season in which roads, campgrounds, sites and trails will be crowded; visiting a park when attendance is low, but the weather good is ideal.

The high season typically is summer, running from Memorial Day through Labor Day weekends; those three-day weekends as well as when the Fourth of July falls on a Friday or Monday, usually draw the largest crowds in a year. In hot desert areas, the high season shifts slightly, as Death Valley and Arches national parks pull more people in late spring and early autumn when temperatures are pleasant.

The ideal time to visit is the off-season just before or just after high season. This can be difficult as usually high season coincides with when children are on school vacation.

Also think about the day of the week you will visit. You usually can avoid crowds by visiting weekdays, especially Monday through Thursday, when attendance dips. On three-day holiday weekends, sometimes the adjoining Thursday or Tuesday can see an uptick as well.

The time of day also plays a role. The earlier in the morning you can get to a national park, the less congested it will be on roadways and at popular sites. Usually, park visitors make their way from the nearest hotels mid-morning to the front gates and then set off again before sunset to their lodging. Note that visitor centers at some parks will close for holidays, usually Christmas.

Of course, visiting during the off-season and on weekdays comes with trade-offs. The weather may be cold or extremely hot; sometimes ranger-led park programs are nil on weekdays, especially in the off-season. In addition, access to some parks can be limited depending on the season. Yellowstone, for example, closes some of its entrances during winter as snowfall at the high elevations makes roads impassable. Other parks, such as Crater Lake, can't be reached at all during the off-season because of heavy snow.

Another possibility for avoiding crowds is to visit national parks that see low attendance overall. Yosemite, Yellowstone, the Grand Canyon and Cuyahoga national parks typically boast the highest attendance so definitely will be crowded during the high seasons. Great Basin (in Nevada) and Theodore Roosevelt (in North Dakota) national parks, however, are easy to reach but see few visitors compared to those in California, Arizona and Utah.

Pets

Pets are an important member of many families, and a vacation with them at a national park is possible, albeit with limitations.

Dogs and cats typically are only allowed in the park's developed areas, such as drive-in campgrounds and picnic areas, but rarely on trails. They also must be on a leash as well.

So if heading on a day hike, what to do with Rover or Queenie? Some parks offer kennels; short of that, one of your party will have to stay behind with the pet.

National forests surrounding the national park usually have more lenient rules regarding pets, so if camping you may want to consider pitching a tent there instead, though an adult member of the party still will have to stay with the dogs while everyone else hikes the national park.

Getting kids involved

Children obviously can benefit from visiting these great outdoors treasures. A trip to a national park will give any child fond memories that will literally last a lifetime. During their visit, they will experience their natural joy of discovery, certainly by seeing and exploring the sights themselves or perhaps through a touch table in which they get to feel fossils or a rabbit pelt at a visitor center. The visit alone will encourage their appreciation for nature. Take them on a hike through these wild areas, and they receive the bonus of exercise in the fresh air.

The National Park Service offers a variety of great, interactive programs aimed at teaching kids about nature through fun and adventure. They often become the more memorable moments of a park visit for children, and a few even give cool souvenirs at the end.

Among the programs:

• **Junior Ranger** – Most parks now offer some version of this program, in which kids by filling out a self-guided booklet and sometimes performing volunteer work can earn a Junior

Ranger patch or pin among other goodies.

• **Ranger-led activities** – Park rangers often host family-friendly activities on the park's geology, wildlife, ecology, history and other topics. Some parks during the evening provide programs in which kids can sit about a campfire and learn about nature.

• **Star parties** – Several national parks, especially those that are remote, offer nighttime viewings of the sky with telescopes. Your kids never will see a sky so brilliantly lit with stars.

• **Touch programs** – Some parks provide kids the opportunity to meet live animals or to touch cool found objects, such as turtle shells, feathers and rocks. They usually are held at the park's nature or visitor center.

Kids' activities aren't limited to just inside the park, however. Before even leaving on your trip, have your children:

• **Check out the park's website** – Many of the websites list activities specific to their park that later can be played on the drive to the park or during hikes.

• **Meet Smokey Bear virtually** – Younger kids can learn about forest fires and nature at Smokey Bear's official website: *www.smokeybear.com/kids*

• **Visit Webrangers** – Get kids excited about your trip with a stop at the Webrangers website (*www.nps.gov/webrangers*). Kids can play more than 50 online games that allow them to explore various national parks.

Hiking national parks tips

Day hiking usually isn't as simple as throwing on one's tennis shoes and hitting the trail. While that may be fine at a small city park, doing so in a national park can invite disaster. Though day hiking hardly requires as much gear or planning as a backpacking trip, you still need to bring some equipment and to think ahead.

Following these 10 simple guidelines should ensure your day hike is problem-free:

• **Know where you're going** – Look at a map of the trail before heading out on it. Bring a paper map and compass with you on the trail and check both frequently as you walk.

• **Get the right footwear** – If your feet hurt, the hike is over. Good-fitting hiking boots almost always are a must on wilderness trails while cross-trainers probably are fine for paved surfaces; sandals almost always are a no-no.

• **Bring water** – You'll need about two pints of water per person for every hour of hiking and even more if in hot or dry climates. Leave soda and sugary fruit drinks at home; they are no replacement for water.

• **Layer your clothing** – Doing so allows you to remove and put back on clothing as needed to suit the weather. Make sure the layer next to the body wicks moisture away from the skin while the outer layer protects against wind and rain.

• **Carry a first-aid kit** – A small kit that allows you to bandage cuts and that contains some emergency equipment such as matches and a whistle will suffice for short hikes.

• **Don't overpack** – A lighter backpack always is better than one full of stuff you don't need. At the same time, don't skimp on the essentials.

• **Use a trekking pole** – Unless the surface you're on is absolutely level, you'll find a walking stick helps reduce fatigue. This is especially true if you're carrying a backpack.

• **Follow the rules of the trail** – Leave no trace by not littering ("Pack out what you pack in.") and by staying on the trail. Don't deface rocks or destroy signage.

• **Don't forget a snack** – Trail mix as well as jerky can help you maintain energy on the trail. It's also a good motivator for any children with you.

• **Enjoy the journey** – Reaching the destination is never as important as having a good time on the way there. If with children, play games, pause when something grabs their attention, and never turn the hike into a death march.

Services and amenities

Services and amenities at national parks can vary greatly depending on the number of visitors and the part of the park you're in. You almost always can expect to find a visitor center and campgrounds with bathrooms; that doesn't mean there will be a restaurant or a vending machine with snacks and water on site, however.

If hoping to stay in a park lodge or at a campground, quickly make reservations; the same goes for hotels, motels and campgrounds near the park. A safe bet to ensure that a reservation can be made is make them at least six months ahead and up to a year in advance at the most popular parks.

Most parks have at least some trails available for those with disabilities to traverse. Be aware, however, that these trails may not head to a park's top sights.

Best sights to see

Which national park trails offer the best vistas? Lead to awesome waterfalls? Let you see wildlife? To enjoy fall colors? Here are some lists of the best national park trails for those and many other specific interests.

Beaches

Come summertime, there's almost no better place to be than the beach. The warmth of the sun upon your face, the sound of waves splashing against the shore, the blue water stretching into the horizon...

Among the most beautiful beaches you can visit are those in national parks. Thousands of miles of shoreline around lakes and along oceans are protected in our parks, and just like the wildlife and rock formations you're apt to find in most of them, the beaches won't disappoint either.

Here are six must-see beaches at our national parks.

Ocean Path Trail, Acadia National Park: Cobble beaches and hard bedrock make up most of the shoreline for the Atlantic Ocean that surrounds the Maine park's many islands. A rare exception is the 4.4-miles round trip Ocean Path Trail that heads from a sand beach to sea cliffs.

Convoy Point, Biscayne National Park: This boardwalk trail is flat and easy, running along the Florida mangrove shore known as Convoy Point. You'll follow the blue-green waters of Biscayne Bay and be able to spot some small, mangrove-covered islands. Bring a lunch; there's a picnic area below palms overlooking the bay. Part of the boardwalk also takes you out over the water. As the bay is shallow and quite clear, you'll have no trouble spotting the bottom.

Swiftcurrent Lake, Glacier National Park: The first 0.6 miles of the trail at this Montana park heads through an evergreen forest with several short spur trails leading to beaches along Swiftcurrent Lake. Meltwater from Grinnell Glacier feeds the lake, making for an crystal clear albeit cold water.

Leigh Lake, Grand Teton National Park: Several alpine lakes perfect for a family outing sit at the Wyoming park's central String Lake Area. The 1.8-mile round trip trail heads around a shimmering blue lake through green pines with gray Mount Moran soaring in the background. During summer, enjoy a picnic on the beach and then a swim in the cool waters.

Ruby Beach Trail, Olympic National Park: The Washington park's Pacific Ocean shoreline features gushing sea stacks, piles of driftwood logs, and colorful, wave-polished stones. To enjoy all three, take the 1.4-mile Ruby Beach Trail. Some of the driftwood here has floated in from the distant Columbia River.

Coastal Trail, Redwood National Park: With more than 40 miles of pristine Pacific Ocean coastline, the northern California park is the perfect place to see tide pools and sea stacks. The latter are visible from many highway vistas but to get close up to a tide pool – a small body of saltwater that sustains many colorful sea creatures on the beach at low tide – explore the 1-mile segment (2-miles round trip) of the Coastal Trail at Enderts Beach south of Crescent City.

Fall colors

Ah, autumn – the world appears to have been repainted, as red, gold and sienna orange leaves contrast with the blue sky. For many travelers, fall is their favorite time to hit the road.

But there's more to see than the leaves. As they fall to the ground, the landscape opens up, allowing you to spot interesting geological features or terrain that summer's green foliage keeps hidden. More animal sightings also are possible as birds migrate while mammals gorge in preparation for winter's cold.

America's national parks offer a number of great places to experience autumn's beauty. And with summer vacation over, many of the parks will be less crowded.

Six national parks particularly deliver great autumn experiences for travelers.

Cuyahoga Falls National Park: Brandywine Falls ranks among the most popular of the Ohio park's several waterfalls. The area surrounding the falls is gorgeous in October beneath autumn leaves, and the Brandywine Gorge Trail to it is shaded

Cedar Creek and Abbey Island at Ruby Beach, Olympic National Park.

almost the entire way by red maples and eastern hemlocks. With a combination of segments from the Stanford Road Metro Parks Bike and Hike Trail, the gorge trail loops 1.5 miles to the falls then back to the trailhead with several crossings of Brandywine Creek.

Great Sand Dunes National Park: Most people visit this Colorado park for the sand dunes soaring 60-plus stories in the sky. There's more to the park than dunes, though. The Mont-ville Trail provides an excellent sample of that as it heads into the surrounding mountains. The 0.5-mile loop partially runs alongside a creek, where the golden canopy of cottonwood and aspen trees sends you to an autumn wonderland.

Great Smoky Mountains National Park: The 1-mile round trip Clingmans Dome Trail heads to the highest spot in the national park and Tennessee. Autumn leaves on the road to Clingmans Dome usually change about mid-October, offering a spectacular red, orange and yellow display. At the dome's top, views of those swaths of harvest colors can stretch for up to a hundred miles in all directions.

Hot Springs National Park: Though hardly thought of as a backcountry wilderness experience, the Arkansas park does offer a number of forested trails to enjoy. The best in autumn is the Hot Springs Mountain Trail. Heading through a beautiful mixed hardwood and pine forest, the route offers a gorgeous fall leaf display – and cooler temperatures than during muggy summer.

Shenandoah National Park: Spectacular autumn views await day hikers on the Stony Man Trail, a segment of the Appalachian National Scenic Trail. At the trail's top, you'll be rewarded with an expansive view of the Shenandoah Valley and the Massanutten and Allegheny Mountains beyond, their trees alit in harvest colors, as you breathe in clean, crisp air.

Death Valley National Park – OK, there are no autumn leaves here at all – but September's cooler temperatures ensure you actually can step out of an air conditioned vehicle for much longer than a minute to experience the forbidding desert landscape. Among the best places in the California park to visit is the Golden Canyon Interpretive Trail, where you can learn to read rocks that tell the tale of how a lake once here vanished.

Romance

What are the most romantic places in the world? Paris? Hawaii? Italy?

Try a national park.

Though national parks often are thought of as places to get back to nature, they're also great spots to get a little closer to your sweetie. Among the romantic possibilities are moonbows, romantic vistas, desert oasis and incredible sunrises.

49 Palms Oasis, Joshua Tree National Park.

Moonbow over waterfalls: At night during a full moon, moonbows often can be seen over waterfalls as the silvery light from Earth's nearest heavenly body refracts off the mist. Plan a spring or early summer visit to Yosemite National Park when the moon is full. On a clear night, moonbows – the moon's light reflected off water droplets – can span 2425-foot high Yosemite Fall with a trail leading right to its base.

Desert oasis: What is more romantic than midnight at the oasis? Joshua Tree National Park has a few, with the 49 Palms Oasis among the easiest to reach. The 49 Palms Oasis Trail heads 1.5-miles to stands of fan palms and water pools. Bring a blanket to lay out on the sand and a picnic basket for an evening snack under the stars.

Breathtaking vistas: For many, vistas of the Blue Ridge Mountains rank among the nation's most beautiful natural

Sunrise at Pu'u'ula'ula Summit, Haleakalā National Park.

scenery. The 4-mile hike up to the summit of Old Rag Mountain via the Ridge Trail at Shenandoah National Park is challenging, but the 360 degree view from the top is unparalleled, as nearly 200,000 acres of wilderness stretch below you. Twirl your beloved around in a dance so that the entire scene spins before her eyes.

Stargazing: Boasting among the darkest skies in continental America, you can see up to 7,500 stars with the naked eye – nearly four times more than is typical in a rural area – at Bryce Canyon National Park. The Piracy Point Trail, a half-mile round trip from Far View Point, leads to a picnic area overlooking a cliff perfect for stargazing. Study up on the names of a few stars in the night sky and point them out to your sweetheart.

Fruitpicking: The Park Service at Capitol Reef National Park maintains more than 3,100 trees – including cherry, apricot, peach, pear and apple – in orchards planted decades ago by Mormon pioneers. For a small fee, park visitors can pick the fruit when in season. While there's no designated trail, the Historic Fruita Orchards Walk takes you through the fruit trees near Utah Hwy. 24. Share with your beloved what you've picked at your next rest stop.

Sunrise to propose by: At 10,023 feet, Pu'u'ula'ula Summit at Haleakalā National Park offers what many consider the world's most romantic sunrise. As the sun ascends over a blanket of clouds below the summit, it colors the crater from the inside out in an incredible light show. Bring a breakfast picnic and as the new day begins, propose marriage, for the sunrise symbolizes the dawning of your life together. Since you can drive to the summit, after she says "Yes," together hike one of the trails into the crater (either the Keonehe'ehe'e Trail or the Halemau'u Trail).

Sunrises and sunsets

Nothing quite so effectively displays Mother Nature's beauty than a sunrise or sunset, those few moments each day when the world shines golden and with incredible serenity.

Some of America's best sunrises and sunsets can be seen in her national parks. They range from the where the morning light first touches America each day to romantic sunsets over tropical waters, from the subtle signal for a million bats to begin their day to incredible sunrises over the continent's deepest chasm.

Here are seven must-see sunrises and sunsets at our national parks.

First sunrise at Acadia National Park: Day hikers can walk to one of the first spots where the sun touches America each morning via the South Ridge Trail in Maine's Acadia National

Park. The trail is a 7.2-miles round trip to the top of Cadillac Mountain, which is the highest summit on the Eastern seaboard. Though the hike would be done in the dark, with moonglow and flashlights, the trail is traversable. Acadia's ancient granite peaks are among the first places in the United States where the sunrise can be seen. Be sure to bring a blanket to lay out on the cold rock and take a seat looking southeast.

Gold-lined paths at Bryce Canyon: Fairyland really does exist – it's smack dab in southcentral in Utah, where a maze of totem pole-like rock formations called hoodoos grace Bryce Canyon National Park. Hoodoos are unusual landforms in which a hard caprock slows the erosion of the softer mineral beneath it. The result is a variety of fantastical shapes. Take the Queens Garden Trail, which descends into the fantasyland of hoodoos. When hiking during the early morning, sunrise's orange glow magically lights the trail's contours.

Bat show at Carlsbad Caverns: About 1 million Mexican Freetail bats live in Carlsbad Caverns. During the day, they rest on the ceiling of Bat Cave, a passageway closed to the public. At sunset, to feed for the evening, the bats dramatically swarm out of the cave in a tornadic-like spiral, their silhouettes stretching into the distant horizon. An open-air amphitheater allows visitors to safely watch the bats' departure in an event called The Night Flight. The Chihuahuan Desert Nature Trail, a half-mile loop, also allows you to watch the bats disperse across the New Mexican desert.

Breathtaking light show at Grand Canyon: Among the Grand Canyon National Park's most spectacular sights – sunrise and sunset – can be seen within walking distance of Grand Canyon Village in Arizona. While the South Rim Trail extends several miles along the canyon edge, you only have to walk to Mather Point, where views of the canyon shift like pictures in a

Hoodoo rock formations at Bryce Canyon ampitheater.

marquee at both sunrise and sunset. Another great spot that's a little less crowded is Ooh Ahh Point on the South Kaibab Trail, which is east of the village and south of Yaki Point. The aptly named Ooh Ahh Point is less than 200 feet below the rim.

100-mile views at Great Smoky Mountains: You can enjoy views of sunrises and sunsets with rays covering up to a hundred miles on the Clingmans Dome Trail in Great Smoky Mountains National Park. How incredible are the sunsets? They can be crowded, as those hoping to photograph the stunning scenery line up 45 minutes before the sun descends.

Romantic sunsets at Biscayne National Park: A full 95 percent of Florida's Biscayne National Park sits underwater, a turquoise blue paradise laced with vividly colored coral reefs – and nothing quite says romance like a sunset over this tropical ocean. Adams Key offers a quarter-mile trail from the dock through the hardwood hammock on the island's west side; most of the route skirts the beach, where the sunset can be enjoyed.

Needles aglow at Canyonlands National Park: Clambering over boulders and ambling across strangely angled slickrock – and watching needles aglow at sunset – await on Canyonlands National Park's Slickrock Trail in southeastern Utah. The 2.9-mile loop trail generally follows a mesa rim. Plan to walk the trail about an hour or so before sunset; on the final mile, tall thin rock formations called needles fill the horizon, glowing crimson as the sun sets.

Vistas

Certainly the best memories of any trip are the great vistas enjoyed along the way. For some, the beauty of the natural scene before them ranks far above any man-made art. For others, the diminutiveness experienced upon seeing an incredible panorama is a spiritual moment.

America's national parks fortunately preserve the most impressive of these vistas. Some offer dramatic desert scenes of changing rock colors while others deliver awe-inspiring autumn rainbows of leaves. One even lets you gaze into an otherwordly basin of hot springs.

Great Smoky Mountains National Park, Clingmans Dome: You can enjoy views of up to a hundred miles atop one of the highest points east of the Mississippi River. The 1-mile round trip Clingmans Dome Trail heads to the highest spot in Great Smoky Mountains National Park and Tennessee and the third tallest east of the Mississippi. The top rewards with an incredible 360 degree panorama. A verdant spruce-fir forest sits at the ridge tops while in autumn the leaves of hardwoods below adds swaths of harvest colors. On clear days, 100-mile views are possible.

Grand Canyon National Park, South Rim: Perhaps the

South Rim, Grand Canyon National Park.

most fantastic vista in all of North America is the Grand Canyon's South Rim. Indeed, the Grand Canyon rightly defies description. Most who see it for the first time say it reminds them of a majestic painting, appropriately suggesting it's a place that only can be visualized by actually gazing at it. While the South Rim Trail extends several miles along the canyon edge, a short section east of the El Tovar Hotel offers the best views. You'll be able to see the Colorado River a mile below and an array of incredible buttes, towers and ridges and that stretch up to 10 miles away to the canyon's other side.

Yosemite National Park, Yosemite Valley: Two sweeping views of Yosemite Valley await on the Sentinel Dome and Taft Point Loop. Located south of the valley along Glacier Point Road, the trail runs 4.9-miles. Taft Point allows you to get right up to the edge of the valley rim, offering magnificent views of

Yosemite Valley below and Yosemite Fall (the tallest in North America) and El Capitan across the way. The 360 degree views from the top of Sentinel Dome – which peaks at 8127 feet – are the hike's highlight. Among the visible sights are Yosemite Valley, Half Dome, El Capitan, Yosemite Falls, North Dome, and Basket Dome.

Yellowstone National Park, Fairy Falls Trail: The multicolored Grand Prismatic Spring and an array of geysers can be seen on the first 0.6 miles of Yellowstone's Fairy Falls Trail. A 400-foot stretch of the trail appropriately known as Picture Hill provides a grand vista of the spring. About 370 feet in diameter, Grand Prismatic is the largest hot spring in the United States and the third largest in the world. It reaches a depth of 121 feet. Be sure to bring polarized sunglasses. By wearing them, you can see the spring's rainbow colors reflected in the steam rising off the water. The smaller Excelsior Geyser Crater sits beyond the geological wonder.

Zion National Park, Canyon Overlook Trail: You can hike past hoodoos to a vista that affords a fantastic view of Zion National Park's famous Beehives, East Temple, the Streaked Wall, and the Towers of the Virgin, on the Canyon Overlook Trail. The 1-mile round trip of pinnacles, arches and domes feels like a walk on an alien world straight out of a science fiction film. Summer temps are cooler in the morning and late evening.

Mesa Verde National Park, Park Point: Park Point, Mesa Verde's highest spot at 8572 feet above sea level with 360 degree views, is often touted as the most impressive vista in the United States. The 0.5-mile round trip Park Point Overlook Trail takes you to the view of Montezuma and Mancos valleys, and on a clear day, you can see four states – Colorado, Utah, Arizona and New Mexico. Add 0.5-miles round trip to the fire lookout tower for additional great views.

Yosemite Falls, Yosemite National Park.

Waterfalls

Nothing quite demonstrates the awesome power and beauty of Mother Nature like a waterfall – hundreds of gallons of water rushing several stories over a cliffside, the vertical stream nestled in lush greenery, the mist and droplets that splash on you at the fall's base.

Fortunately, several of our national parks preserve many of the country's most fantastic falls. Most of them are quite easy to reach via short hikes.

Yosemite Falls: If there is one waterfall that everyone absolutely must see, it's this one in California's Yosemite National Park. Actually consisting of seven waterfalls, Yosemite Falls sends water rushing 2,425 feet downward into the valley. Depending on snow melt, the falls' peak flow typically occurs in May when up to 2,400 gallons of water flow down Yosemite Falls every second.

You can hike 1.2-miles round trip to the base of North America's tallest waterfall. During spring, you may want to take the trail on a clear night when the moon is full, especially if on a romantic trip. Moonlit rainbows – called moonbows – span the waterfalls.

Queenie and Fido also can enjoy the waterfalls, as leashed dogs are allowed on the trail. Be sure that your dog is comfortable with crowds and other people, however.

Tokopah Falls: Not many travelers have heard of Tokopah Falls, but it's an incredible sight. A series of cascades, it drops 1200 feet – almost the height of the Empire State Building – at California's Sequoia National Park. It's a park of tall trees and tall waterfalls. A glacier carved Tokopah Valley, leaving high gray cliff walls that cradle a meadow, creeks, and a pine and fir forest. The 3.8-mile (600 foot elevation gain) Tokopah Falls Trail leads to its namesake, which is the park's highest waterfall.

Avalanche Lake waterfalls: With melting glaciers and high mountains, waterfalls can be found aplenty in Montana's Glacier National Park. Melting glaciers feed several lakes across the park, including Avalanche Lake. Start on the Trail of the Cedars then turn off onto the Avalanche Lake Trail. The 4.7-miles round trip (505-foot gain) trail heads to Avalanche Lake, where several waterfalls from Sperry Glacier drop several hundred feet to fill the valley with its turquoise waters.

Hidden Falls: You can enjoy this waterfall and then a vista at 7200 feet elevation on Grand Teton National Parks' Hidden Falls-Inspiration Point Trail. The trail runs 3.8-miles round trip into Cascade Canyon. Though technically not a waterfall but a series of cascades running 200 feet over several multiple steps, Wyoming's Hidden Falls still impresses. Because only part of the cascades are steep, there's a lot of confusion among various sources about exactly how high the drop that looks most like

Hidden Falls, Grand Teton National Park.

a waterfall actually is – some say 80 feet and others say 100. Afterward, visit Inspiration Point, a short walk from the falls.

Fairy Falls: The trail to Fairy Falls at Yellowstone National Park offers a three-for-one deal: the multi-colored Grand Prismatic Spring, an array of geysers, and a 197-foot waterfall. If going to see Old Faithful, this is a perfect nearby trail to hike the same day. The 5.6-mile hike begins with geysers then arrives Grand Prismatic Spring, a wonder that boasts multicolored rings of algae. Fairy Falls comes next. The waterfalls' base supports a variety of vegetation. If looking for a place to picnic, the rocks downstream from the falls where raspberry bushes grow makes a perfect spot.

Marymere Falls: A trail through a lush, old growth forest that ends at this waterfall will delight anyone hiking the Marymere Falls Trail at Olympic National Park in Washington. The 1.6-mile round trip trail really is like taking two entirely different hikes in one. Most of the trail heads through an intensely green Pacific Northwest rain forest while the last portion at the destination is purely about the waterfalls. Marymere Falls is about 90 feet high, and you'll get really close to it as the trail passes the small plunge pool. Hikers also can take a stairs to see the falls' upper segment. A few landings on the stairs offers fantastic views of the falls from different angles.

Laurel Falls: Though Rainbow Falls is the tallest at Great Smoky Mountains National Park, many visitors pass it up because of the strenuous hike. One that's much easier to reach and still spectacular in its own right is 80-foot Laurel Falls. The Laurel Falls Trail runs 2.6-miles round trip through a pine-oak woods with hemlock and beech along the stream, making for a colorful walk in autumn. May also is impressive, as mountain laurel blooms along the trail and near the falls, which runs its highest that month. Deer, often with fawns, wood squirrels, and songbirds are common on the trail. The waterfall on Laurel Branch consists of an upper and a lower section. A wide walkway crosses the stream where the mist from the falls roils overhead.

Brandywine Falls: This 65-foot waterfalls awaits visitors on the Brandywine Gorge Trail at Ohio's Cuyahoga Valley National Park. The Brandywine Gorge Trail loops 1.5 miles to the falls then back to the trailhead with several crossings of Brandywine Creek. The area surrounding the falls is gorgeous in October beneath autumn leaves, but the trail can be hiked any season. It's shaded almost the entire way by red maples with eastern hemlocks and green moss upon the ground once closer to the falls.

Wildflowers
From rare California poppies to sweet-scented phlox, wild-

Catawba rhododendron blooms, Great Smoky Mountains National Park.

flowers begin to bloom each spring across much of the country. Filling green meadows, desert basins, and forest floors, wildflowers bring a special beauty that usually can only be seen for a few weeks.

Our national parks rank among the best places to enjoy wildflowers. As those parks cover wide swaths of protected land, they offer ample area for massive blooms, enhancing the already beautiful scenery.

Here are six not-to-miss spots at our national parks for spotting wildflowers from March through summer.

Pinnacles National Park: Each spring, brilliant orange California poppies, lavender-colored bush lupine, and white mariposa lilies blossom across the nation's newest national park. To see a variety of them at different elevations and from a number of vistas, take the High Peaks and Bear Gulch trails.

Great Smoky Mountains National Park: About the same time on the other side of the continent, the forest floor on the Mingus Creek Trail turns fragrant with the pleasant sent of blue phlox. Several other shade-loving flowers also can be found along the creek, including violets, Virginia bluebells and white trillium. During late April, expect to see flame azalea in bloom on the Deep Creek/Indian Falls trails. In May, look for mountain laurel, and in June for rhododendron.

Glacier National Park: From late June through early August, summer wildflower blooms are at their peak. Check out the Swiftcurrent Lake Loop Trail for meadows strewn with purple asters, white torch-shaped clusters of beargrass, and sun yellow glacier lilies, all with majestic mountains as a backdrop.

Sequoia National Park: Next to the world's largest trees are blossoms that somehow manage to stand out despite their comparative size. On the Crescent Meadow Trail in early July, lavender Mustang clover with yellow centers look like little pins of brilliant light against the immense pine cones that have fallen into the grass.

Crater Lake National Park: Wildflowers usually bloom along the stream next to the Annie Creek Trail and across the meadows from mid-July through August. Among those that might be spotted are Macloskey's violet, big huckleberry, sulphur flower, Crater Lake currant, western mountain ash, and wax currant.

Great Basin National Park: Amid the high desert is an oasis of summer wildflowers on the Alpine Lakes Trail. Spring-fed Lehman Creek flows into a lake and supports Parry's primrose, penstemon, and phlox, all set against vibrant green grass. Butterflies are abundant here as well.

Wildlife
America's national parks are known for their great vistas and fantastic rock formations, but they also preserve another treasure: wildlife.

Bison at Lamar Valley, Yellowstone National Park.

In fact, national parks rank among the best places to see interesting and rare wildlife. Late summer marks a particularly good time for wildlife viewing at many parks as most mothers bring out their young that time of the year.

Given the breadth of national park locations, there's also the opportunity to see almost every kind of North American wildlife, from those that live on mountains, in marine environments, and in the tropics to those that make their homes on prairies, deserts and in temperate forests.

Mountains: Travelers can explore the "Serengeti of North America" on the Lamar Valley Trail at Wyoming's Yellowstone National Park. Like the mountain-ringed African plain, Lamar Valley serves as home to the classic megafauna that define North America. Bison, elk, grizzlies, black bears, wolves, coyotes, eagles, osprey and more all can be found at this high elevation. Coyotes also can be seen wandering about, looking for a meal while bald eagles and osprey grace the skies. Grizzlies reside in the hilly woods, but they and the area's other big two predators – black bears and wolf packs – prefer to remain under cover than be seen.

Marine: You can encounter an array of marine wildlife on the Beach Trail at Alaska's Glacier Bay National Park. Low tide also provides an opportunity to see intertidal life. As the waters retreat into the ocean – and water levels here can fall 25 vertical feet, among the greatest extremes in the world – a number of animals and plants are exposed. Don't be surprised to spot starfish and snails on the sands and grasses. On shore, a variety of sea birds gather and fly over, often nabbing exposed intertidal creatures for a meal. During those first moments of sunlight, watch for humpback whales, harbor porpoise, puffins, sea otters, and Steller sea lions, frolicking and feeding in the mouth of the bay. Bring binoculars. If lucky, you'll also hear the blow of humpback whales.

Tropics: Tropical wildlife can be safely seen from the Anhinga Trail at Florida's Everglades National Park. The trail's boardwalk takes you over open water where you can watch for alligators peeking out of a river, as well as turtles, herons and egrets. Winter marks the best season to see the most wildlife. A number of birds spend their time in the Everglades after migrating from a northern clime. Among those you can spot are the double breasted cormorant, great egret, great blue heron, snowy egret, tricolored heron, white ibis and woodstork. Turkey vultures congregate in the marsh during the early morning hours.

Prairies: North America's largest mammal – the bison – freely roams North Dakota's Theodore Roosevelt National Park, and the Buckhorn Trail is an excellent place to spot them and other Great Plains wildlife. The trail includes a prairie dog

Gila woodpecker, Saguaro National Park.

town that stretches for about a mile. You'll be able to spot them barking from their burrow entrances as they keep an eye out for predators. Hawks, coyotes and rattlesnakes are among the creatures hoping to make an unsuspecting prairie dog its dinner.

Deserts: Four desert ecosystems can be found in North America, and the park closest to a major metro area offers among the best spots to see wildlife of these dry climes. Outside of Tucson, Ariz., Saguaro National Park's Douglas Spring Trail crosses the Rincon Mountain District (Saguaro Park East), providing the chance to see coyotes, roadrunners, jackrabbits, quail and Gila woodpeckers. All five of those creatures thrive in the Sonoran Desert, which stretches across Arizona and northern Mexico, as well as good portions of the continent's other three desert ecosystems.

Temperate forests: Great Smoky Mountains National Park, though stretching across the Appalachian Mountains, offers the opportunity to see many of the animals that reside in temperate forests covering much of the continent east of the Mississippi River. The Deep Creek/Indian Falls trails in the park's North Carolina section sports Eastern cottontail rabbit, groundhogs, river otter, and white-tailed deer. Also present but much more elusive, as they keep to themselves, are black bear, bobcat, coyote, red fox, red wolf, and wild boar.

Winter

Most travelers think of summer as the best time to hit national parks – but winter also offers several spectacular sights that make for memorable visits.

So when the snow starts falling, consider a road trip to one of the following parks.

Birders paradise: Winter marks the best time to hike Florida's Everglades National Park, as the subtropical climate means unbearably hot and buggy summers. Indeed, a number of birds already know this and spend their time in the Everglades after migrating from a northern clime. Among those you can spot on the Anhinga Trail are the double breasted cor-

Golden Canyon, Death Valley National Park.

morant, great egret, great blue heron, snowy egret, tricolored heron, white ibis and woodstork; turkey vultures congregate during the early morning hours.

Wildlife sightings: Leafless trees and snow's white backdrop makes sighting large wildlife a lot easier in winter than summer. The Warner Point Nature Trail on the south rim of Colorado's Black Canyon of the Gunnison National Park offers the chance to spot elk and Rocky Mountain bighorn sheep. Look for the elk in clearings and the bighorn sheep on the rocky cliff sides.

Heavy waterfalls: At most parks, waterfalls are most active in spring and early summer, thanks to snow melt. Not so at Washington state's Olympic National Park. Rain is more likely there during winter, meaning the water flow is higher, making for a more spectacular creeks and falls. One good trail through the park's lush, old growth forest that ends at a waterfall is the Marymere Falls Trail.

Bearable heat: During summer, oppressive heat makes California's Death Valley National Park at best a pass through seen from a motor vehicle. The park's average high in January is a pleasant 67 degrees, though, making winter the perfect time to walk the foreboding desert landscape. Among those sights is the lowest point in North America. Badwater Basin sits 282 feet below sea level and can be accessed in a mile-long round trip hike.

Avoid the crowds: Visitation drops during winter at most parks, so the trade-off for bundling up in coat, cap and gloves is seeing the great scenery without all of the crowds. A good bet is Yosemite National Park's spectacular Yosemite Valley in California. The Lower Yosemite Fall Trail offers a number of fantastic views of Yosemite Falls in a 1.2-mile loop with the added coolness of falling water frozen in mid-flight on the granite rocks.

Christmas

A little secret: Among the best ways to escape holiday stress is a national park trip. Though often thought of as a summer destination, only a couple of the parks close in winter, and almost all offer warm, cozy and peaceful holiday experiences. A bonus is that almost all parks are less crowded during winter.

Here are five great holiday-themed must-do's at our national parks.

Winter wonderland, Yellowstone National Park: Book a getaway at the Old Faithful Snow Lodge, which can only be reached this time of year by snow coach or snowmobile. The Christmas-decorated lodge keeps its fireplace burning with plenty of hot cocoa for visitors. During the day, hike past "ghost

Christmas caroling in the cavern, Mammoth Cave National Park.

trees," formed when the steam from the Old Faithful geyser freezes on pine tree needles. Bison with snow-covered manes often feed across the geyser valley.

Polar Express train ride, Cuyahoga Valley National Park: Each December prior to Christmas, the Cuyahoga Valley Scenic Railroad's Polar Express chugs through the scenic Ohio park. Among the highlights on the refurbished passenger train is a reading of the children's book "Polar Express," which inspired a movie and this trip. Many passengers ride the train in their pajamas! If in the Southwest, a private company also runs a Polar Express to Grand Canyon National Park.

Luminaria-lit skiing: Denali National Park: Every December, rangers light the small paper lanterns that line ski trails at the Alaska park. Visitors also can snowshoe or stroll the route, which leaves from the Murie Science and Learning

Center, Denali's Winter Visitor Center. Several other National Park Service sites offering luminaria displays and hikes including Florida's De Soto National Memorial and Arizona's Tonto National Monument.

Snowshoe wildlife hike, Rocky Mountain National Park: Ranger-led snowshoe tours take visitors of this Colorado park to a variety of wildlife, including elk, coyotes, deer and snowshoe hares. The trail is utterly quiet as snow-capped mountains and evergreens rise around you on all sides.

Caroling in a cave, Mammoth Cave National Park: In early December, the Kentucky park holds Christmas carol sing-ing in the world's longest cave system. It's a tradition that goes back to 1883 when local residents held the first Christmas celebration in the cave's passageways.

Historical sites

While the National Park Service's 61 major parks largely focus on protecting natural wonders and wilderness, they also preserve several historical sites. Though many are merely ruins, others are in just as good of shape (if not better) than when they originally stood.

Historic Fort Jefferson: At Dry Tortugas National Park, you can visit a fort used during the Civil War. Built with more than 16 million bricks during the mid-1800s, Fort Jefferson is the Western Hemisphere's largest masonry structure. Six walls and towers with a moat make up the fort's outer area on Garden Key.

19th Century Mining Town: Crossing a thick rolling woodland, the Colorado River Trail at Rocky Mountain National Park offers nice views of Colorado River, arguably the Southwest's most important waterway. The trail to the ruins of an 19th century mining town, Lulu City, in a 6.2-miles round trip with 320-

John Oliver cabin in Cades Cove, Great Smoky Mountains National Park.

foot elevation gain.

Appalachian life: A number of great day hikes allow visitors to explore the Great Smoky Mountain National Park's rich history. Pioneer cabins and mills await on several short day hikes, including those at Cades Code and Mingus Mill.

Butterfield Stage station: Along the Texas-New Mexico border, you can step back into the Old West and experience the remoteness of what once was a welcome sign to travelers: a Butterfield Stage station in the Guadalupe Mountains. The 0.75-mile round trip Pinery Trail marks a great day hike for families at Guadalupe National Park. The trail leads to the ruins of the Pinery Station, a once favored stop on the original 2,800-mile Butterfield Overland Mail Route.

Trees

Among the most fantastic sights at our national parks are

trees. Whether they be gigantic, fossilized, or older than the hills (figuratively speaking), they're certain to awe. Here are six great tree sites to visit.

Sequoias: Your family will feel like hobbits walking through scenes from "The Lord of the Rings" movies on the General Grant Tree Trail at Kings Canyon National Park. The 0.5-mile trail heads through the General Grant Grove of giant sequoias. More than 120 sequoias in the grove exceed 10 feet in diameter and most tower several stories over your head.

Redwoods: Hiking families can enjoy a trip into what feels like the forest primeval on a segment of the Damnation Creek Trail in Redwood National Park. For those with younger children, a 1.2-mile round trip through just the redwoods section of the trail makes for more than an incredible, inspiring walk.

Bristlecone pines: On several of Great Basin National Park's glacial moraines rise incredibly ancient bristlecone pines, many nearly 5,000 years old, meaning they began growing as the ancient Egyptians built the pyramids. The 2.8-mile round trip Bristlecone Pine Trail allows you to walk among a grove of the trees, which scientists say likely are the oldest living organisms on Earth.

Joshua trees: Day hikers can enjoy a walk through a large Joshua tree forest in the desert above the Palm Springs, Calif., area. A segment of the Boy Scout Trail at Joshua Tree National Park runs through a grove for a 2.4-mile round trip. Technically not a tree, the unusual Joshua tree is a member of the lily family.

Chestnut trees: Day hikers can head through what used to be a grove of majestic chestnut trees. The Cades Cove Nature Trail runs 1.4-miles round trip trail (from the parking lot) and sits in Cades Cove, an isolated mountain valley that is a popular destination thanks to many well-preserved structures from

Base of General Grant Tree, Kings Canyon National Park.

pioneer days. A few seedlings of the great chestnut remain.

Petrified forest: Families can hike the remains of a woodlands dating from the dinosaurs' earliest days on the Great Logs Trail in Petrified Forest National Park. The fairly easy walk consists of two loops that combine for a 0.6-mile round trip. Because of the hot Arizona weather, spring and autumn mark the best time to hike the trail.

Learn more about these and many other great national park trails in the author's "Best Sights to See at America's National Parks."

About the Author

Rob Bignell is a long-time hiker, editor, and author of the popular "Best Sights to See," "Hikes with Tykes," "Headin' to the Cabin," and "Hittin' the Trail" guidebooks and several other titles. He and his son Kieran have been hiking together for more than a decade. Rob has served as an infantryman in the Army National Guard and taught middle school students in New Mexico and Wisconsin. His newspaper work has won several national and state journalism awards, from editorial writing to sports reporting. In 2001, *The Prescott Journal*, which he served as managing editor of, was named Wisconsin's Weekly Newspaper of the Year. Rob and Kieran live in Wisconsin.

CHECK OUT ALL THESE GREAT HIKING BOOKS BY THE AUTHOR

"Best Sights to See" series:
- America's National Parks
- Great Smoky Mountain National Park
- Indiana Dunes National Park
- Rocky Mountain National Park
- Voyageurs National Park

"Hikes with Tykes" series:
- Hikes with Tykes: A Practical Guide to Day Hiking with Children
- Hikes with Tykes: Games and Activities

"Headin' to the Cabin" series:
- Day Hiking Trails of Northeast Minnesota
- Day Hiking Trails of Northwest Wisconsin

"Hittin' the Trail" series:
National parks
- Grand Canyon National Park (ebook only)
Minnesota
- Gooseberry Falls State Park
- Split Rock Lighthouse State Park
Minnesota/Wisconsin
- Interstate State Park
- St. Croix National Scenic Riverway
Wisconsin
- Barron County

- Bayfield County
- Burnett County (ebook only)
- Chippewa Valley (Eau Claire, Chippewa, Dunn, Pepin counties)
- Crex Meadows Wildlife Area (ebook only)
- Douglas County
- Polk County
- St. Croix County
- Sawyer County
- Washburn County

GET CONNECTED!

Follow the author to learn about other great trails and for useful hiking tips:

- Blog: *hikeswithtykes.blogspot.com*
- Facebook: *dld.bz/fBq2C*
- Pinterest: *pinterest.com/rbignell41*
- Twitter: *twitter.com/dayhikingtrails*
- Website: *dayhikingtrails.wordpress.com*

If you enjoyed this book,
please take a few moments to write a review of it.

Thank you!

Made in United States
Orlando, FL
16 October 2023

37960221R00074